Field Manual

Warriors of YHWH
Order of Melchizedek (Prophets)
Order of the Culdee (Chaplains)
Order of the Gate (Knights)

Abbot-Bishop David Michael, OC, OG, ThD
Abbot General

Glentivar Village Press
POB 464, Tombstone, AZ. 85638
glentivar.org
ISBN # 978-0692708804

Second Edition 1.4 with 2017 Updates
Fully Copyright Protected
July 4, 2013 with update March 16, 2016

Prologue

It pains me to have to write this kind of a book. However, I see the coming Satanic oppression meant for America and the rest of the world and have no other recourse. In all cases, mercy should always be offered <u>before</u> judgment is pursued in battle. It is the nature of YHWH through Y'Shua to extend mercy to all of mankind before he will bring judgment upon a person, people or a nation.

I am of the advanced age where I would like to stand on the sidelines while sending the young and skilled into battle. But this is not what will happen. The engagement described in this book has evolved into a biker brotherhood called the Sons of Prophets to fight the forces of Satan. This is first a spiritual battle in the heavenlies that will be seen in physical battles on earth.

The forces of Satan as the Dragon of Revelation will seek out to destroy all who stand in the gap who side with the mission of the warriors of YHWH. What appears to be occurring in this age is a call to knighthood with all of its fanfare and excitement is really a call to be prepared for martyrdom.

Those who are called as warriors as Knights and who embrace the following protocols will be fighting some of the most powerful beings and creatures yet to be 'released' upon the face of the earth. It is only an 'abiding' faith in YHWH and the forgiving mercy of Y'Shua that will make any victory possible. It is only the humble purity of heart and the desire to extend mercy to others that will protect a Knight from the mortifying sword of the enemy.

We have the promise that in the final battle, truth and righteousness will prevail and the Kingdom of YHWH as ruled by King Y'Shua will be established on earth.

To those who are called as warriors of YHWH, should they (you) accept this mission, be assured they (you) will be assisted by legions of angels. It is good for every knight and every Christian to remember, "Blessed are the meek for they shall inherit the earth."

In this updated publication, I have included the dream-vision of the rise of the 7th Legion of Septimania who once served Rome. This Legion is being raised up in America as the warriors of YHWH for these end times. Please read this dream-vision carefully and pray that the Lord Y'Shua shows you your mission in these last days.

May the Lord YHWH be with you in power and might. So be it!

Contents

1. History of the Orders

We shall begin by visiting the origin of this mission as I have experienced it. This is my journey in and out of the domain of the Beast now being led by Pope Francis who is a Luciferian and conducts Satanic masses in the Vatican as a Jesuit.

Warriors of YHWH

The warriors of YHWH have multiple origins as the fighting corpus of the Order of Melchizedek, the Order of the Culdee and the Order of the Gate. In my personal family history as a hereditary member of the Templars for the last 800 years is significant.

The Templars once protected the hereditary line of King David but now, this has been satanically corrupted. While I was serving within the Roman Church as a Syro-Chaldean Deacon, the Order of the Gate was founded under Pope John Paul II in 1986 and I made its Abbot.

Protection of Jerusalem

The call of the Syro-Chaldean can be traced back to the time of King David to first Antioch and then to Jerusalem when in 1000 BC the warrior armies of Israel were trained to fight against the Canaanite Nephilim who had invaded the land of Palestine. This Order was a military order created in the protection of Holy Jerusalem.

Tracking the ownership of Palestine back, Palestine was given to Noah, then to Shem and then to Abraham, then to Jacob (Israel) and then to King David and finally to Y'Shua by YHWH since 4000 BC at the beginning of Adamic human history. These Hebrews are a different people group than most of the modern Edomite-Turkish (Khazar) Jews who live there today.

It was mandated by YHWH for King David to finally regain the capital city of Jerusalem (then called Salem) that had been the capital under Shem the son of Noah who was first called the Melchizedek. Shem as the Melchizedek blessed Abraham before destroying Sodom and Gomorrah assisted by the angels of YHWH.

Order of Melchizedek

The Order of Melchizedek is the primary hereditary priesthood over the earth and the cosmos. It is this priest-king-prophet appointment that is empowered to bring judgment and offer blessing and mercy. This Order cannot be granted by man as done by the misguided Mormons but can only be given by YHWH.

Battle Against the Nephilim

In this battle against the Nephilim Sodomites, there is evidence of nuclear devastation in the Sodom and Gomorrah region still lingering in the soil to this day. King David was the first to say that those as warriors of YHWH who remained behind to guard the provisions would get the same 'pay' as those who fought in battle. He was a man of equity and assured justice for all Israelites.

David's sons became a warrior priesthood in their own right paralleling the priesthood of Aaron established by Moses. It is biblically recorded that the Aaronic priests also called the sons of David 'priests' in understanding this parallel Melchizedek priesthood. This Davidic priesthood continues to thrive in full power to this day as the Sons of David continue to be the YHWH appointed protectors and guardians over Israel and its people scattered throughout the earth. This is the remnant of the Melchizedek priesthood.

Praise the Lord with harp: sing unto him with the psaltery and an instrument of ten strings:

Psalm XXXIII. 2

King David established the origin of what became the Hebrew Blue Tunic Warriors and by the time of King Arthur in Scotland and in France who were called the Swan Knights in the 6th century and then by the 8th century where known as the Knights of Calalus in the Americas.

These warriors would continue to be tasked to protect Jerusalem and the royal genetic line of the throne for the rightful King of Jerusalem and its outlying lands which included America.

Jerusalem Throne

The only rightful King that may sit on the throne of Jerusalem is Y'Shua who is the current living hereditary King of Israel. Y'Shua is the Melchizedek and is the ruling high priest and king over all the earth and the cosmos. All others who may claim to be king or presume to have authority over the lands of Israel (Palestine) are mere impostors and pretenders.

Recent Papal Affirmation

Being this as true, in 1986 the Order of the Gate as a part of this line was recognized within the personal Prelature of Pope John Paul II then called the Catholic Apostolic Church / International Ordinariate operating under the Canons of the Syro-Chaldean Church.

I was ordained into this Papal Prelature as a Deacon in November of 1985 and was given the title as the Protector General of Jerusalem. This mission was called the Order of the Gate and served then under the apostolic seal of Mar (Bishop) John Dunnigan of this Papal Prelature. This mission has evolved into the Federation of Jesus Abbeys. http://jesusabbeys.org

Empress Blessing

In 1998, Abbot David was acknowledged by signed letter as the Abbot General of the Order of the Culdee by Lynda Von Habsburg who is the Papal crowned Empress of the Holy Roman Empire circa 1960.

At the time, this mission known as the Order of the Culdee was a religious order of 'Hebrew-Celtic Christian' priests and brothers who spiritually oversee mission of the fighting Order of the Gate. This Order of the Culdee is the Celtic name for the Order of Melchizedek translated as the "Friends of God" or Theophilus in Greek.

I was at that time in 1996 accepted as the Wing Chaplain of the Civil Air Patrol in Hawaii, the Congress established Auxiliary of the USAF. Today Culdee chaplains continue to encourage Knights of the Order of the Gate to fulfill their spiritual mission. Many of these Chaplains are descendants of the family line of King David of Jerusalem. Some are also Melchizedek priests or prophets as called by YHWH in to this mission.

Antichrist Rome

After 25 years working with the Vatican on a task force created by Pope John Pail II, I know full well the inner workings of the Roman system, both spiritual and temporal.

The Vatican of the Roman Catholic Church as ruled by the Jesuits are determined and destined to provide for the rise of the Antichrist, the False Prophet (Pope Francis) and the Beast who will war against messiah Y'Shua and his armies.

America in Prophecy

We also know America will be used by the NWO (Jesuit subordinates) to become the primary military power in forcing the rest of the world to worship the image of the beast.

The current illegal shadow government of America will become the two-horned beast described in the book of Revelation in the disguised form of a two headed eagle. This empowerment is traced to its origin through Rome, Greece, Egypt, Babylon and then to Sumeria where the two royal sons of King Anu, Enlil and Enki, of the Anunnaki claim to be the creators of man. It actually goes back further to a lost civilization once existing now underwater in the Persian Gulf.

Marduk (Ra), the son of Enki is the current ruler of this advanced human-like alien species originating from fallen angels in now claiming to be the rightful god over the earth's human races. Above him is Lucifer who has not yet fallen to earth but will in the middle of the 7 year tribulation period as described in the book of Revelation and the book of Daniel.

America Divided

The two-horned (two headed) Beast described in Revelation in chapter 13 is America after it has gone through an economic collapse and is raised from the dead by the NWO as a two headed or horned political nation – just as the two-headed phoenix raises from death in myth.

The Western America will be ruled from the Denver (Airport underground facilities most likely) area whereas the Eastern America may likely be ruled from an underground facility in North Carolina near Asheville.

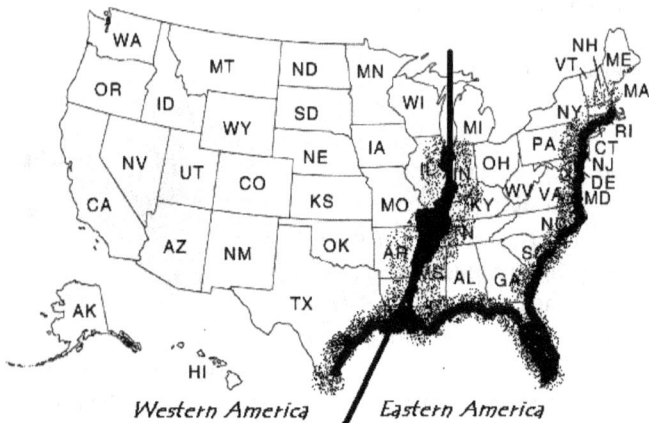

Western America | Eastern America

America Army of Satan

United Nations NWO

America will then be used to force the rest of the world to worship the image of the beast of Europe which is the 10 headed, 7 horned Holy Roman Empire. The 7 horns of the Holy Roman Empire are the 'Nephilim' spawned royal houses of Britain, Spain, Portugal, France, Germany, Switzerland and Italy that will become the bond-servants to the reign of the False Prophet, Antichrist and the Beast. These 7 royal houses will divide the world up into 10 regions by reclaiming the lands or colonies they once held mostly circa the 19th century.

Habsburgs

The Hapsburg's of Austria as the primary royal house of the 7 houses will retain the title of Emperor and Empress over the others as the Holy Roman Empire. It is the head of the house of Hapsburg who holds the title as King of Jerusalem. He who holds Jerusalem as the most sacred place holds the world.

Warning

Being these things are true, it is necessary that the warriors of YHWH be prepared for the rapid shifting of the balance of power in a rapid and radical shift in political-economic systems of the world before they happen. Money in the bank and banks in general will be frozen when this occurs and this may only take 48 hours to happen according to experts.

Food and fuel will be severely rationed and travel across county lines may be blocked. The division of America is likely to happen in conjunction with the event of the New Madrid Fault giving way thus geographically dividing America in two down the Mississippi basin. I would not want to be near the Mississippi when this occurs.

Pray to YHWH to seek to know exactly where you are to be as we move into this cataclysmic shift of world power and assets. I can only say is can happen most any time now.

2. Mission Directive

The mission directive for the Warriors of YHWH is derived from the most ancient Order of the Melchizedek also known as the Culdee among the Celts and the Theophilus among the Greeks. The meaning of the terms is simply, "Friend of God."

A version of this as the Order of the Gate dates to 1985 and carries the Seal of Mar (Bishop) John Dunnigan who was the bishop and mentor of Abbot David. The original Mission Directive reads as follows:

~~~~~~~~~~~~~~~~

The Order of the Gate (Eastern Rite)

It is hereby declared:

Through the Holy Spirit and under the jurisdiction of the Hebrew Christian scriptures, creeds and traditions of the followers of Y'Shua Hamashiach; the Order of the Gate is sent of God by vision and prophecy as confirmed by the following signate of ecclesiastical authority to entreat the monotheistic world to prepare for the Messiahs return.

Whereas:

The Order of the Gate is sent as a spiritual army in the disciplined 'Worship' of God [YHWH] to establish His Kingdom on earth and the release of His anointed ones. Whereas:

The Order of the Gate looks to Jerusalem as the City of the coming Messiah and to the ancient King's Gate in the east wall as the 'station' we guard in prayer and passive* resistance against the many false-Christs that will come.

*passive only as it is possible to remain so and still fulfill the mission.

Whereas:

The Order of the Gate accepts into its ranks married or celibate persons of any denomination that will take the vow of 'Guardian of the Gate' as the protectors of the 'Liturgy of the Tabernacle' and of the 'Kings Gate'.

Whereas:

The Order of the Gate shall establish schools, libraries and hospitals whenever and wherever possible to teach the love of God [YHWH} through the methods of prophetic inspiration (communication arts), teaching of history (language and culture) and the mastering of practical technology (nutrition, energy, water, and shelter [NEWS]).

Whereas:

The Order of the Gate will look to God [YHWH] as the supplier of all financial needs as we work with our own hands to fulfill this call. Gifts will not be solicited, nor will there be a financial structure to embrace them. Institutions brought into being by the order will seek an accountability to local ecclesiastical authority.

Whereas:

The Order of the Gate will look to local and renewable natural resources as the energy source for meeting local energy needs in accordance with natures law of self-regeneration.

Seals of Authority

Seals on original document by the hand of Bishop Mar John of Segan, Catholic Apostolic Church, International Ordinariate in 1986 as delivered to Abbot David Michael (then ordained a deacon in the CAC/IO). Mar (Bishop) John originates from a long line of Oriental Catholic Bishops of Syria (Syro-Chaldean) that were both priests and princes of their people.

The Catholic Apostolic Church was at the time recognized as valid by Bishops of Oriental, Orthodox, Roman, Anglican and Celtic Apostates. Mar John was granted title as the titular Bishop of Iona in 2005 by Patriarch and Archbishop John Stanley of the Syro-Chaldean (Aramaic) Church and passed this on to Abbot David at his passing.

"When the grass disappears, the new growth is seen, and the herbs of the mountains are gathered in" (Prov. 27:25).

If we were to simplify the mission of the Sons for Prophets, it would be contained in the following simple statement.

"Prepare, Conquer, Occupy and Defend"

Our Mission

This is our mission against the darkness that is to soon enslave America. It is in response to the soon fall of America's economy, political system and vast infrastructure that we exist. We will need to build self-reliant outposts.... a fully separate self sufficient food producing camps for the remnant of the faithful.

In essence, some of the Warriors of YHWH are to become bike riding 'Preppers' as popularized by television and other media. In time, a mule or horse may take the place of a Harley. This is the mission we may effectively present to the general public whenever asked. Other missions as presented in this Manuel are for us to know among ourselves alone.

This Manuel was not originally written for public distribution but was a private printing originally written for the members of the Order of the Gate, the Order of the Culdee which is a tasked company of the Order of Melchizedek with its support network. It is not that this book has hidden knowledge but that it can confuse those who have not been initiated into the bigger picture of the forces at play in these end times.

For many the open discussion of demons, aliens, fallen angels and their Nephilim offspring is deeply disturbing. It causes many to fear because they do not know the power of YHWH, his heavenly angels and his angelic-alien allies.

Pursuing with the public an open discussion of the political-economic fall of America is more palatable for most Americans as they intuitively know our culture is coming to an end.

With our presence as bike riding Preppers as being our highest public profile, it will also include the establishing of Healing Cafe's run by the Chaplains of the Culdee that will reach out to the general public in touching the lives of the needy to bring them into our camp.

3. Code of Chivalry

The code of chivalry was romanticized by the French during the Crusades. It emerged as a guide for encouraging the purity of knighthood beginning circa the 8th century as the Crusades were mobilized and continued throughout the crusader period well into the 17th century. The core idea was that for God to judge justly between you and another in battle, your own heart and life had to be pure and sinless before God.

The 10 Commandments were the original principles in the development of the code of chivalry. In brief, these commandments are:

1. Obey YHWH (God).
2. No Idols.
3. Honor YHWH's name.
4. Keep the Sabbath (Saturday).
5. Honor Parents
6. Do Not Murder.
7. Do Not Commit Adultery.
8. Do Not Steal.
9. Be Honest.
10. Do Not Covet.

These 10 Commands evolved into various codes of honor emboldening such battle cries as: "Protect the innocent"; "Oppose the greedy"; "Dispatch the infidel"; "For God and the Church" and; "Fight until victory or death."

The bonds of friendship and trust were well reinforced in most orders of knights during the Crusades where they had to depend upon their fellow knights for their survival in battle. Their strength was in the unity of numbers with all fighting as a well oiled machine as a single unbreakable line of force.

The heavy horse charge of knights common with medieval knights was almost unstoppable by any defensive line from the 8th through the 16th centuries. Our heavy horse today needs to become the warrior angels of YHWH as the point team in wielding the forces of nature. I have thus far at the time of this writing been approached by both the angelic generals of the winds (Michael) and of Fire (Uriel) in this regard with a promise to assist.

To be considered a man of chivalry, you had to know much more than just how to fight and survive. Music, dance, poetry, history, politics, economics, religion, technology and philosophy were all considered necessary knowledge and skills to be an honorable man of chivalry.

A man's personal bearing had to be one of benevolence. This benevolence was well played to the ladies at court and to the troubadour musicians who would write of the many godly deeds of the knights of chivalry. We however as warriors of YHWH seek to become insignificant that Y'Shua might be greater in the eyes of our enemies.

The dress of the knight was of the highest fashion if possible and his armor of the latest design. He knew well the manners expected of a gentleman and gave honor to whom honor was due in the class system of the day.

In the peace-time games of military skill, a knight would often be seen giving mercy to his fallen opponent. The offer of mercy was always a forerunner to judgment in play as well as in war. It showed the knight was committed in representing a loving God of mercy and not a mindless God of judgment. However, if the terms of mercy were not accepted by the defeated, death would be swift and merciful.

The Code of Chivalry was the guiding light for many centuries during a time when the Church and Crown were inclined to discourage learning and the liberty of thought. This cannot be so for the warrior of YHWH.

In due time, the Code of Chivalry became the ethical principle that became the honorable way of conducting modern business and commerce in the Western world. We see this carried into business ethics although case law has undermined this simple justice of common law ethics.

4. Becoming a Knight
Preparation

To become a knight, a man must first be proven. As a man embraces the code of chivalry, he is then tested for truth and honor in the many battles of life.

Knighthood is commonly conferred by a nobleman who has some place of honor in the courts of a royal house or is a royal himself. In the case of Saul and David becoming kings, this act of conferring kingship was done by the prophets. This is still the highest form of transfer of honor and mission over and above the so-called divine rights of royal houses.

In modern times, most all royalty in Europe make claim to be descended from the line of King David but sadly most of these are descended from Nephilim yDNA genetics. Thus, knighthood for the Orders here is the setting apart of those committed to the mission of King David. Today for these Melchizedek orders, it is conferred by prophets.

Ritual of Knighting

Knighthood occurs in a divine ritual before YHWH that confers knighthood with the tapping of the blade of the sword upon the shoulders of the one to be knighted. It also includes a baptism of water and fire where one is knighted into the Order in the name of the Father, the Son and the Holy Spirit as a witness of his vows. A 3-day fast is often conducted by the one to be knighted that he might purify himself in body, soul and spirit in the sight of God and seek God for his life's noble quest as a knight.

Taking the Vows

Vows are made by the knight to uphold his Faith in YHWH in adherence to the rules of the Order along with a vow of obedience given to the leadership of the Order.

The words spoken by the Abbot General or his representative who is a verified prophet may simply be the following.

> Do you vow to uphold the 10 commandments that guide the Knights of the Order of the Gate even unto death?
>
> *I do ... even unto death.*
>
> Do you vow to obey the directives of the Abbot General of the Order fo the Gate in the measure that your conscience allows you even unto death?
>
> *I do ... even unto death.*
>
> "I, _____ confer knighthood upon thee in the name of the Father and the Son and the Holy Spirit as your witness and power over evil. Arise Sir _____ and greet your fellow knights in arms.

After knighthood is conferred, the new knight will then be given the tunic of the Order with the Orders symbols embrazened over the heart of the knight. A belt and sometimes spurs were also given. The belt of truth was given to keep him from evil as 'holy unto God' and spurs were given in symbolizing his desire to walk in peace.

Non-Combatants

Those who are not called to be fighting knights may be called by God to one of the Orders as a non-combatant. For such members seeking priesthood as a sacred teacher, it is the Order of the Culdee to which they will join and they then become the chaplains to the Warriors of YHWH.

Others not called as knights or priests may become sergeants to support the mission in providing food producing farms, manufacture of needed supplies and in prayer. The same vows apply to all three levels of status with the prevailing principle of "laying down your life for your brothers" as paramount. Such a sacrifice is captured in the words of Y'Shua.

"Master, which *is* the great commandment in the law? Jesus said unto him, Thou shalt love the Lord thy God with all thy heart, and with all thy soul, and with all thy mind. This is the first and great commandment. And the second *is* like unto it, Thou shalt love thy neighbor as thyself. On these two commandments hang all the law and the prophets."

Matthew 22:36-40

Greater love hath no man than this, that a man lay down his life for his friends.

John 15:13

5. Rank and Protocol

Three Primary Ranks

The Order of the Gate as Knights herein described have thee primary levels of rank including the rank of Knight, Sergeant and Soldier.

The Sergeants and Soldiers serve under a Knight as a single battle unit. Above the Knight is a Knight Commander who leads a Commandery of up to 12 Knights and above the Knight Commander is the Abbot General of the Order of the Gate (knights) and Order of the Culdee (priests).

Rank Insignia

The insignia of rank for the Knight is a single star. For this Knight Commander is 2 stars and for the Abbot General is 3 stars. The Command Sergeant's rank insignia is three chevron stripes. For the Tech Sergeant it is two chevron stripes and for Soldier class it is a single chevron stripe.

Abbot General

Knight Commander

Knight

Command Sergeant

Tech Sergeant

Soldier

Titles of Address

It is the custom when in a formal gathering to address others of the rank of Knight or higher with 'Sir' prior to their first name. The Abbot General can simply be addressed as Abbot.

Promotion

Knights can promote anyone of their men under their command up to the rank of Command Sergeant. Some consideration should be given to time in rank but ultimately, it is the achievement of skill and knowledge that is the justification for promotion. A training program should be in place in every unit to encourage the men to pursue promotion.

The requirements in the level of skill and knowledge achieved for a promotion should be clear to members and awarded without personal favoritism.

The rank of Knight is conferred by the Abbot General or by a Knight Commander if given this 'right of proxy' in writing by the Abbot General. Knight Commanders are promoted to positions over a Commandery only by the Abbot General.

6. Uniforms and Armor

Field Armor

For the Sons for Prophets, there are field uniforms and armor and there are parade uniforms and armor. When gathering for events of honor or celebration, the parade uniform and armor is to be worn as appropriate. If in training or deployed on a mission, field uniforms and armor are to be worn as appropriate.

Field armor varies with the conditions of the mission. The standard field uniform is a black tactical uniform with tactical vest and tactical helmet. Camo may also be used in rural wilderness conditions. Biker Commanderies may continue with the traditional biker black leather uniform.

If seeking a covert identity, every effort should be made to reduce the possibility of reflecting light from any part of the uniform. It should be loose fitting enough to provide a full range of motion in hand to hand combat.

Weapons and ammunition should be located on the vest and elsewhere that is easily accessible and will not hang up when crawling through debris and other obstacles.

It would also be noted that the vest should provide a first-aid kit, a survival kit, emergency food and water and an approved communications device.

Armor of metal or ceramic plates may be added to the exterior or interior of the uniform to increase the survivability of the knight but in so doing, it will create a more obvious signature that can be identified by advanced electronics.

Keep in mind the key objective is stealth and a knight is to hit the assigned target before the enemy knows what is happening. He is to be gone before the enemy has a chance to identify location and return fire.

Stealth

Becoming invisible within your environment is paramount as stealth is your greatest friend in this mission. Keep this in mind in all uniform choices.

Parade Armor

Parade uniforms and armor may be somewhat medieval in appearance and are determined by the Knight Commander as appropriate.

Parade armor of medieval styling normally consists of a tunic with crest, belt, high boots, pants, gloves and hat or helmet. Show armor may be added such as shoulder plates, breast plates and forearm plates. Parade armor may also include capes and lances with banners to showcase the discipline and honor of the Knights of the Order of the Gate.

It is advisable that all knights enter training for Equitation specifically in dressage and quadrilles to become proficient riders.

The purpose of parades is to show the unified brotherhood in a commitment to each other and to the mission of the Order. In this the many become one in battle. It is also to show the skill that would be carried into battle if needed by the show of discipline of horse and rider.

As an alternative to the horse, a Commandery are permitted to ride motorcycles in the same manner in the show of discipline and unity. This is a great recruiting tool that is encouraged whenever this is possible.

7. Stealth & Silent Weapons

The mastery of silent weapons will save the life of a knight in battle. Assault rifles with noise silencers are the preferred primary offensive weapon. Other silent weapons may include the knife, crossbow, blowgun, Taser, sword and throwing stars. For long distance, a sniper rifle up to a 50 caliber with silencer may be used with appropriate ghillie gear to hide the snipers location.

The art of stealth is critical to disabling your target before you are identified as a threat. Methods used to block the human signature are vital to survival considering the efficiency of advanced personnel sensor systems now commonly used in the field by military.

A knight must employ efficient methods to hide or disguise the, 1) human body heat signature, 2) block any metal signature, 3) alter the human form signature, 4) mask any noise or color signature different from the surrounding environment and, 5) block the signature that comes from using electronics.

These methods for assuring maximum stealth are all vital to surviving and completing the mission.

Stealth does not always mean you should not be seen. Disguises are very effective in hiding the intent of your mission and personal identity. This means one can be hidden in plain sight and walk through most any hostile environment undetected.

Hiding in Plain Sight

Dressing up with makeup as an old lady or man hunched over using a cane to walk will often persuade the enemy you are not a threat and you will be ignored.

Other possible disguises my include dressing as a bicyclist, clergy, mechanic, utility repair person, security guard or other peace keeping or public service uniform or even a drunk or street person. You are in stealth when your presence as seen is to be expected and those watching do not consider you to be a threat.

If you are to assume a disguise, it is recommended you be seen in the area weeks before you intend to engage your target. Appear as if you have just moved into the area and are now a resident. Associate with some of the locals and be seen in conversation with them.

In suburban and city areas, cameras are being placed at every street corner with face recognition software providing super computer analysis speeds. You will be seen and there is no way around this.

Be prepared to be seen as someone you are not rather then who you are. Be ready to change your disguise if you think you are being considered as a suspect and being targeted to be watched.

8. The Enemy

The enemy in these final wars on earth are not altogether human. The fact is the Warriors of YHWH are being trained to fight alien, evil angel, demon and Nephilim entities who appear to be human but who are not. Some will not appear to be human in some cases.

The truth is the primary enemy will not be of the seed of Adam and will not be in the employ of YHWH. However, they may be of the seed of Eve as coming from the line of Nephilim Cain and/or Nimrod or others. The book of Enoch is the best reference for the 'Watchers' who are fallen angels coming to earth both before the flood and after the flood in taking the daughters of men and spawning a hybrid race of evil Nephilim.

Y'Shua has come, died and was resurrected to put an end to any question of who is God and provides to us the power to be overcomers in battle.

Alien Enemy

Aliens really include any species of intelligent life who were not born on earth. Many of the known species are fallen angels who have taken on a form (shape shifters) that best fits the environment where they live. Enoch states the fallen angels or Watchers are Shape Shifters in that they can take on different bodies, genders and looks. These species may include the Reptilians, Grays, Andromadans, Pleiadians, Nordics, Lemurians .... and more. Many of these species have extremely advanced technologies.

Some in this field of alien research have identified at least 23 different species of alien who now live on earth and interact with various governments and shadow organizations.

Some of these species are the enemy of YHWH in siding with the great Seraphim dragon (draconians) who is the biblical Satan and Lucifer.

Other aliens are friendly to the survival of the human race of the seed of Adam that began in the Garden of Eden. They are our allies. The great challenge for the Knight is knowing the difference.

It is currently believed that most all of the Reptilians and their subordinate Grays are opposed to the survival of the seed of Adam. It is also understood that some of the Pleiadians, Atlantians and the Anunnaki have a secret alliance with the Reptilians in giving alien knowledge and technology to empower the rise of the NWO regime under that Seraphim Dragon called Satan with the Anunnaki as the ancient offspring of this Seraphim with RA as the current warlord NOW on earth.

The ability to clearly know what alien species is the enemy and who is a friend is not clear at this time. It can only be revealed by the revelation of the Holy Spirit of YHWH. It will likely be on the field of battle that the true nature of the enemy is finally revealed. However, those sensitive to the revelations of the Holy Spirit of YHWH as prophets will know before this time and will be prepared to confront the many deceptions as they emerge.

It is known that the Illuminati (world bankers), the Royals of Europe of the Merovingian blood lines (7 nation royals) and the Papal throne (via the Jesuits) are in support of the rise of the NWO. It is also understood that these alien demigods will have an unquestioned rule over the earth and over all the groups above as their royal man-god vassals. So the battle is a global and even a cosmic battle involving every species that exists.

Evil Angel Enemy

The species of evil angels is in identifying the fallen angels who originally took the daughters of men from which the Nephilim were born.

In the book of Enoch, there were 20 leaders of these evil angels identified by name. See the book Prophets II for an in-depth understanding of this. What is interesting is they had the ability to shape shift taking on the genetics of different species and to then procreate with their offspring being very much a physical being like Adamic mankind. Many of these fallen 'Watchers' were imprisoned in the Abyss in the Euphrates but will be released soon. See dream at the end of this book.

It is believed that many such evil angels walk the earth today and some may even be your close neighbors. This is not stated here for you to become afraid. We must remember; "Greater is he (the Holy Spirit of YHWH) that is within you than he that is in the world."

What is distinctive about evil angels is they hate true Christians with a passion and are of reprobate minds. This means they cannot hear the truth since their minds and lives are beyond redemption. They do not appear to have a conscience and they do not give value to moral laws and authorities. Many of them are cannibals and eat human flesh in rituals to gain power over Adamic humans. Be watchful for them.

They are known to kill Christians who do not have the protection of YHWH. Again, vampirism and cannibalism are known to be common activities in the evil angel societies. They tend to associate with those of their own species and you will usually find them living close together in spiritually 'dark' neighborhoods.

Nephilim Enemy

The Nephilim are the offspring of human women and male evil angels. They may also be the offspring of other alien species and human women providing the alien species if compatible with the genetics of human procreation.

31

Some aliens are experts in genetic engineering and can 'create' a human-alien hybrid with science that is also of a Nephilim type species. It is common for Nephilim to take on a dominant nature of evil in their lives such as murder, cannibalism, sexual depravity, sodomy and other crimes against YHWH and Christian society.

Because they are half human and half 'god' in being above man in power and intelligence, they are compelled to make claim over the lives of humans in dominating human societies and people groups throughout history.

Notable Nephilim leaders in history appear to have included Cain, Nimrod, some of the dynasties of Pharaohs, Goliath, Charlemagne and others. Both the Merovingian royals of Europe and the 13 families of the Illuminati bankers claim a very high percentage of yDNA Nephilim blood.

Most of these families trace their first paternal origin back to Cain as the first Nephilim whose father was Sama-el and mother was Eve. They as a god-man species consider themselves to be gods over the rest of the human world who only exist for their good pleasure and the pleasure of their evil angel fathers.

Demon Enemy

According to Enoch, when a Nephilim dies, their spirits not being human are bound to wander earth until the time when Y'Shua will finally gather them up, judge them and cast them all into a place of no return. They are called evil spirits with the male offspring being demons and the female offspring being sirens.

One demon during the day of Y'Shua asked why he had come before the end of time to torment them? The evil nature they embraced when in body as a Nephilim they continue to try to live out by invading and possessing the soul and body of humans and even animals be able to again express their perverted passions in a physical body.

Y'Shua asked what was their name. They said they were called 'legion' which is over 2000-6000 demons in one man. Y'Shua then cast them out of the demon possessed man and sent them all into a herd of pigs. This spiritual intrusion for the pigs was so traumatic that it caused them to run blindly over a cliff where they all died. The demons were then left to wander the 'dry places' until they could find another human or animal host.

Human Enemy

There will be many misguided humans who will side with the NWO and the Satanic regime in the final battles. It says in the Scriptures that most of the human world will be deceived and take the Mark of the Beast and join his armies against Y'Shua and against the true Christians.

It is important to consider the degree of bondage a human is in before dispatching them to await judgment. If they have taken the Mark of the Beast, their destiny is set and death is their best deliverance from a far worse eternity in hell. In this case, it is a mercy killing. Yes...this is an act of mercy and not murder.

Power Over Evil

What can we do to dispatch alien enemies, the evil angels, the Nephilim, demons and the cooperating human enemy? For a Knight of YHWH, four of these are human-like in that they can die from a mortal wound.

In this, the skill to battle with weapons is important. Demons and higher fallen angels are not human and must be neutralized by the Melchizedek priests who work with the command of Michael the Archangel who has as many as 720,000 warrior angels divided into 12 legions.

Sword the Last Weapon

I am of the personal belief that there will come a time when high technology weapons will be ineffective and only the literal sword will be left to be effective against certain evil entities. In a dream, I was shown the Sword of Goliath that was for killing the Nephilim (included at the back of this book). A Knight should be trained in the sword but clearly understand that it is YHWH who gives the victory in battle with the help of his angelic armies.

Behind everything that is evil in this physical world, there is a spiritual reflection that is more real than what we see. It is from this spiritual world where the enemy draws power directly from the great dragon who is Satan himself. To weaken your enemy, a knight must pray the prayer of separation to break the conduit of evil power from Satan to the enemy you are fighting. This is a spiritual link that has to be broken.

String Theory

This may not make sense in the natural realm but it is associated with the concept of 'string theory' in science. It says two locations in space at any distance can be fully interconnected with an <u>instant</u> exchange of energy, power, thought, expertise and even a super-spiritual entity who would appear to be co-existing in both places at the same time.

Without this spiritual break of power between your enemy and Satan, you would be fighting the power of Satan himself. In Scripture, it is only Y'Shua who has the purity to bring Satan to his knees. Even Michael the Archangel said the "Lord Rebuke you," to Satan when debating over the body of Moses so as to not bring himself under judgment in the courts of heaven.

Satan still has much power in the heavens (cosmos) and he is to be respected even though he uses this power for evil. Soon Michael in war against Satan backed by Y'Shua will drive him out of heaven and he will 'fall' to the earth and realize his time is short.

When the enemy armies including aliens, evil angels, Nephilim and demons have fallen, then Satan will be cornered, captured and chained for 1000 years by Y'Shua himself.

However, it is for us as the warriors of YHWH to bring down the armies of Satan as YHWH would lead us to do so. After this resistance will come the 144,000 Hebrew prophets also known as the Order of Melchizedek who will continue in this battle on earth. During this time, Y'Shua arrives to earth with his heavenly armies after the defeat and fall of Satan from the heavenlies.

Spiritual Armor

To be prepared to fight, a knight must have his spiritual armor well mounted on his spiritual being. If the battle is physical, he must be prepared for battle with weapons appropriate to the mission.

The Armor of God found in Galatians 6 includes:

1. Cloak of Obedience.
2. Helmet of Salvation.
3. Breastplate of Righteousness.
4. Belt of Truth.
5. Shoes of Gospel Peace.
6. Shield of Faith.
7. Sword of the Spirit.

A knight must also carry the Mark of YHWH in his life. One such mark of this is the keeping of the 10 Commandments including the Saturday Sabbath.

He must also take on the nature of YHWH daily in embracing the redeeming principles of the Tabernacle of David found at the end of this Field Manual.

Finally, a knight must overcome the enemy by the purity of the blood of the lamb covering his own sins and he must operate in the word of his testimony in a life of prayer, chastity, poverty (not seeking personal wealth) and obedience. More on this is to be found in the book, "2015 Nephilim Wars."

9. Our Alliances
Alien Allies

Some of the potential allies who are alien are sill deciding with whom they will ultimately side. They will be forced to side with either Satan also called the Great Dragon or with YHWH and his son Y'Shua. There will be no other option and no fence sitting in these final battles.

Although I have stated that some of the Pleiadians, Atlantians, Anunnaki and Reptilians have formed an evil alliance under the Great Dragon (Draconian), this may not apply to all of these species.

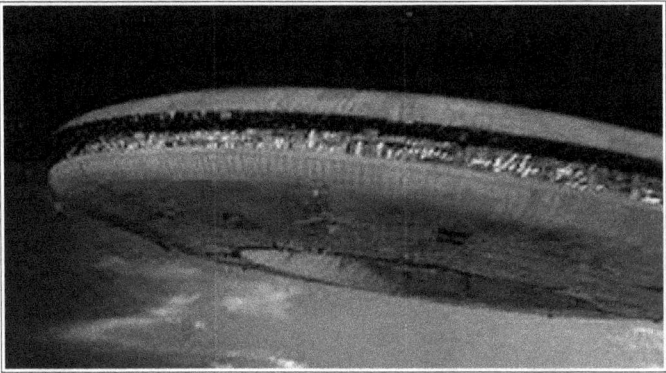

However, my experience with the Andromadans has always been positive as they provided 'transport' to me to see some of the events that are yet to happen in the future. This was an event of time travel as best I understand it. I also saw in the spirit a great armada of thousands of massive Andromadan mother ships (miles across in size) and smaller support ships travel through space toward earth in early 2012. I was then told, "The Andromadans are coming" by an angel of YHWH.

I have every reason to believe they are committed allies to the cause of YHWH. However, this does not preclude the possibility of a faction of them rebelling and forming an alliance with the Draconian enemy.

We have to become extremely sensitive to the leading of the Holy Spirit and let the spirit within us bear witness with any entity group. We must have a deep spiritual peace with any spirit or being before we embrace them as friends. If they are friends, it will ring true within our spirit since we have the Spirit of YHWH.

If they are not, there will be a deep apprehension even though they may say all the right words and appear to give us aid in battle and even lend to us their advanced technologies.

Angelic Allies

It is clear in Scripture that the angels in the employ of YHWH are our allies. In fact, there are possibly 720,000 warrior angels of great stature associated with the 4 winds under the command of Michael the Archangel.

I was told this in 2012 and the full story is in the book, "2015 Alien Invasion" and in the book "Prophets I." I will provide just the conversation here that I had with Michael the Archangel. The letter 'D' below in the conversation is for David (me) and 'M' is for Michael the Archangel.

D: Why was it said, "With this cross you will conquer?"
M: It is the symbol for the four winds. I will give you the 'protection' of the 4 winds. They are an army.
D: Is that why I was called 'Windwalker' by the angels in a dream where I looked down upon the earth and traveled through the solar system?
M: Yes. This name and call was known to them some time ago. Music will be the language to speak to the four winds. You have had this prophetic 'music' gift since your fast upon Mount Zion when you were age thirteen. It is for this reason that the 'wind' angels have sang with you in worship on many occasions.
D: How many are there in the army?
M: Twelve legions of angels are assigned to the four winds.
D: How are they structured as an army?
M: There are 4 Generals leading each wind and they are represented to man in dreams and visions in the form of horses that often speak. You met one of them in 1982. The four winds are represented as companies of red, black, white and dappled horses.
Each wind has three Captains under the four Generals with one legion of angels assigned under each Captain. The 12 Captains under the 4 Generals have taken the names for each of the 12 tribes of Israel.

D: What about the staff that I have proposed?
What kind of material should be used for the coil
tip or focal point?
M: That which transcends time and matter.

Angels of War

Most angels of war are of the highest species
created and are interdimensional and can function in all of
the 12 dimensions of space and time. It says in Scripture
that Adamic man was created a little lower than the angels
but through redemption in Messiah, he will become the
judge of angels. In this, Adamic mankind will in time be
ranked above angels in species by YHWH in this capacity.

In reference to the above conversation with
Michael the Archangel, his angels have power over the
winds to bring judgment upon the earth and against the
regime of the Satanic NWO. This angelic army will side
with the Knights and the priests of Melchizedek

Scriptures showing their realm of power are as
follows.

- Four winds are represented as horses of four
  different colors. Zec. 1
- Wind horses travel the earth assessing the state of
  peace or war upon the earth. Zec. 6:5
- Angels have a charge to protect us. Ps. 91:11
- The Son of man sent forth his angels – angels
  under his command. Mat 13: 41
- Twelve legions available to aid the cause of
  Y'Shua and the Saints. Mat 26:53
- Angels gather the elect from the four winds. Mat
  24:31
- We (sanctified man) will judge angels. 1Cor 6:3
- Four angels [generals] are given the command
  over the winds. Ez 6
- Angels are ministering spirits sent forth to
  minister (serve) the heirs of salvation... Heb 1:4

- Be hospitable... you may entertain angels unaware. Heb 13:2
- Four Angels (generals) over four winds holding them back. Rev. 7:1
- Twelve angels have power to hurt the earth in battle. Rev. 7:3
- Told to prophecy to the four winds to breath life into the slain. Ez 37:9
- Winds come from the treasure trove of God. Ps 135:7, Ps 18:10
- Four winds cause earthly kings/kingdoms to rise or fall. Dan 7:2
- God causes his winds to blow. Ps 147:18, Ps 135:7
- God gathers the wind(s) in his fist. Prov. 30:4
- Winds can divide the seas. Is 11:15
- God will rebuke the nations with the winds. Is 17:13
- Winds thresh the mountains [earth]. Is 41:15, Is 57:13
- Wind can ravage the walls [fortresses] with water, fire and hailstones. Ez 13:13
- The wind carries away the broken iron and clay (Antichrist alliance) crushed by Y'Shua. Dan 2:35

Human Allies

The human allies are those who have not taken the Mark of the Beast or bowed to the Image of the Beast. They are committed to YHWH as his servants. Y'Shua has been made their Lord and King and they follow him to the best of their understanding even to death.

I should mention that those who are inclined toward the ideals of socialism will in time take the Mark of the Beast. I would suggest you not associate with them but avoid them whenever possible. Socialism can take two major forms.

Fascism and Communism are common ideals in the world today. All of those in these camps will be deceived and fall under the enslavement of the Beast.

Those who uphold the liberties of the US Constitution may be considered allies but they should be tested and proved before any information of the Order is provided to them. Ultimately, the only YHWH form of government is a Constitutional Monarchy with the Bible as the Constitution and Y'Shua as the crowned King. The testing of humans is also like testing aliens in that it is primarily a spiritual process.

10. Rules of Engagement
Communications

The rules of engagement is the manner by which you engage the enemy in battle. This would also apply in information (intelligence) gathering and in any relationship with the enemy.

In many wars of the past, there has been a protocol of communications agreed upon by both sides so as to reduce the degree of the mass devastation of life and property. Once a communications protocol has been established between enemies, this should be honored.

I continue to nurture an open communication with certain people who I consider strategic to the rise of the NWO associated specifically with the Holy Roman Empire and the occult priesthood of the NWO. We hold most of the facts related to an alien active presence on earth in common.

The Nephilim living among us claim to be demigods and of the blood of the creators of humans. What then is human? However, we greatly differ on who Y'Shua is and who is the rightful God over the many human civilizations of earth.

I have been accused of dabbling in the occult because of this open communication but I find this necessary to better understand what powers are at work in the world and who is pulling the strings from behind the scenes for world events to occur. This information I have tried to reveal with clarity in the 2015-17 series of the four NWO books I have recently published.

Why the War

The wars of the future are not driven by rational people or by rational alien demigods. Wars today are not accidental or the result of limited oil resources or for humanitarian aid or defense. The ultimate goal is world domination even to the control of souls with what is thought and perceived.

Further, these wars are really intended by evil to remove any threat of the Adamic priestly line of King David ever ascending to a position of power over the civilizations of earth.

The rival priesthood of evil comes from the line of Cain backed by his father Sama-el also known as Satan and the great Seraphim Dragon. This NWO Satanic regime will not stop in war until there is not one male left of the seed of Adam who genetically carry the male yDNA royal line of King David in their blood.

Defeated by Innocent Blood

I know of those of the Davidic line living today who are being targeted by the NWO to die at their hands if/when YHWH allows this. Until then, they remain protected by YHWH and his angels. The call of knighthood is really a call to death as a martyr as the ultimate victory over evil. Those who "live by the sword will die by the sword." This law of war must occur.

You as a Knight will most likely die as a martyr of YHWH should you accept this mission when it is your time set by YHWH. You should fully know that it is the shedding of innocent blood, your blood, that will secure the final victory over Satan and shorten the time to the day of judgment for him.

The more people Satan kills who walk in righteousness before YHWH, the more his power is drained from him and the days of the war and human destruction are shortened. This is a spiritual law of cause and effect that he cannot be revoked.

However, if Satan can compromise our faith through temptation and get us to sin and then kill us, he avoids all judgment in this killing since your death is then justified due to sin.

Jesuit Agenda

I can tell you that the Jesuits as a priesthood of the NWO hold to the same 'rules of engagement'. They are avowed assassins and many a righteous man and women in the thousands have died at their hands over the last 400 years.

Now that Pope Francis as a Jesuit has full authority in uniting the papacy and the Jesuit 'black pope' agenda, they will now move more freely and quickly in fulfilling their hidden mission in the world.

You will see great peace and unity come by the hand of Pope Francis but this is just a prelude effort in unifying the world religions under the Roman Catholic Church. The strategy is to give dissenters of the Roman church what they want, bring them into the regime with their vows of fealty and then the Jesuit Vatican will separate the subordinate from the rebellious. They will then eliminate the dissonant people.

Dividing of the Denominations

The Protestants are now secretly committing to Rome in accepting the Pope as the "first among equals" and the "Vicar of Christ" on earth. Protestant denominations sheepishly give Rome power to be the judge over them. In doing this, they can no longer be given the protection of YHWH and of the Melchizedek priesthood.

The members of the World Counsel of Churches and all 501c3 churches will give this kind of fealty to Rome or loose their standing as churches and denominations in the world governments. If they do not, their ministers will be discredited and their not-for-profit resources confiscated by the NWO regime in compliance with Jesuit Rome.

Only the children (servants) of Rome will be permitted to survive into the NWO regime which sadly will include most of the Protestant and Reformation denominations existing today. It will also include the Muslims, Buddhists, Hindus and all other religions.

A Satanic trinity will be common in all of the world religions. It will be based on a father god, a divine mother and a child as the messiah on earth. Every religion has this Trinity including Christianity with God, Mary (the theotokos – mother of god) and Jesus as a messiah. The only difference is that YHWH will become Lucifer but the title of Jesus and the Holy Spirit will not change. In the Islamic trinity, there is Allah, Buraq (the feminine expression of Allah also expressed as Fatima, Sophia and Mary) and then Mohammad his prophet and a messiah.

Islamic prayers verify this illicit secret worship of the Divine Mother.

A Sufi Ode to the Divine Mother

On the face of the earth there is no one more beautiful than You.

Wherever I go I wear your image in my heart.

Whenever I fall in a despondent mood I remember your image.

And my spirit rises a thousand fold.

Your advent is the blossom time of the Universe.

O Mother you have showered your choicest blessings upon me.

Also remember me on the Day of Judgment.

I don't know if I will go to heaven or hell.

But wherever I go, please always abide in me.

11. Tracking & Surveillance

More than Footprints

The skill of tracking is vital when seeking to put your self in the advantaged position in battle. If you can analyze your target's habits, associations, their hangouts and vices, you are already moving into the offensive position. One should always be in the offensive position as this is the position of YHWH in all things.

Tracking today is more than following foot prints in the dirt and associated signs to discover the trail left in the wilderness by a target. Today, it also includes using the computer, casual interview techniques, systematic observation and electronic sensor surveillance to gather strategic information.

We are not concerned here about any 'privacy act' since the US Government and NWO shadow organizations all ignore such claimed human rights. However, the devices that we may employ should not be traceable to you or the Order. This is a real challenge since proprietary electronics can often be traced to locations and sometimes even people by its components and design characteristics.

Sensor Devices

I taught digital electronics, PIC programming and robotics for 5 years at a tech college and designed many inexpensive devices that can gather information about people. I worked briefly for DAARPA (US Aerospace R & D) in sensor development with MIT and the University of Hawaii in developing various surveillance devices we hid in fake rocks smaller than a baseball for deployment in Afghanistan. These devices were reported to be dropped out of planes and completely networked. If one or more were destroyed, it did not effect the 1000's of others also deployed in the area.

What we do need is generic easy to carry sensor devices for gathering information as intel for the Knight. The idea is to silently protect the parameter surrounding your camp by up to ½ mile. Sensors may include the following:

- PIR sensors
- Motion sensors
- Ground vibration sensors
- Light beam sensors
- Proximity sensors
- Switch sensors
- Sound / voice sensors
- Micro-radar sensors
- TV/Video micro cameras
- Form (geometric) sensors
- Metal sensors

Micro Computers

A pre-processing device (PIC computer) can fit into a small pocket or even a lighter and the signal from these senors can be encrypted and transmitted from the PIC computer to other devices. The primary processor may be no more than a PDA or smart phone (with GPS disabled). Ultrasound and infrared communications may also be employed for sensor communications. The output device options could result in causing the following pre-programmed events:

- Explosive devices.
- Projectile devices.
- Sound/siren devices.
- Door locking / caging devices.
- Scent or color marking devices (UV ink spray).
- Smoke or tear gas devices.
- EMP microwave devices (disables electronics)
- Non-lethal personnel neutralizing devices

Disposable stealth silent surveillance devices need to be used extensively by stealth warriors. These should be used in complement with the age-old methods of 'sign' tracking in the wilderness or urban environment to identify the threat and its location.

EMP Concerns

With concern for EMP for these devices, it is recommended that non-transistor devices be developed to prevent being fried from EMP. EMP is now considered imminent. It is not an 'if' question but a 'when' question by US agencies. There is some research being conducted by the Order in the development of static charge switching devices that would not be effected by EMP. Enough said on this. Switching high voltage relays may also be used as an alternative to EMP volatile transistor switching.

12. The Horse
Why the Horse

The biker's horse is the motorcycle. If this fails (no fuel), we will have to resort to the live horse as our transport. This chapter provides some basic training information for riding the horse. The horse has been the friend of man for over 6000 years and is still viable today in modern warfare. The advantage today is seen in Afghanistan where the mountain Afghans have never been overcome by either the Russian Armies or the US /NATO armies.

They used the horse to move quickly though the rocks and ravines of the mountains to position themselves for a 'sniper' attack and then before the invading forces are able to locate them and retaliate, they are gone. The land is such that vehicles are not effective and men on foot cannot hope to catch the mounted Afghans.

This advantage only works if the defending force , the Afghans in this case, are able to choose the best offensive positions also suitable for the horse. It is my understanding that our future battles against the NWO will be in the high mountains and deserts that will become our chosen offensive and it will be the horse and mule that will become the most effective in human transport. In these mountains, caves will need to be identified to provide cover for the Knights with their horses in avoiding electronic sensor systems.

The primary mountains for these battles in the US include the Rocky Mountains, the Ozarks, the Appellations and the Adirondacks. Some of the desert 'badlands' found on Native reservations will also be the chosen location for such battles.

We have to choose our offensive positions long before a confrontation occurs since we likely will be severely outgunned by an extremely superior force with aircraft, missiles and deployed NWO military personnel.

These offensive positions should not ever be mapped but memorized with food, water and equipment stores buried for future use.

The Saddle

After many years of riding both Western and English, I find the Western Saddle too heavy and stiff for military riding. I prefer a more forward seat closer to the withers of the horse with less leather separating me from the horse. I have come to prefer an Australian saddle. Cross country and barrel riding saddles also work.

The saddle being more forward on the horse enables the horse to turn more easily by being less constrained in the back. Such saddles also tend to be lighter than common Western roping saddles which enables more speed from the horse in a fast charge or retreat.

I also prefer a deep seat with high cantle and knee pads to stay in the saddle while freeing both hands if needed for fighting. A horse can be trained to turn by sensing a shift of weight to the forward left or right combined with leg aids.

The training requirement is for the horse to sense your change of position in the seat and thus respond to these changers as a command (aid) very quickly. For this reason I recommend an Australian saddle or other deep seat saddle for the warriors of YHWH.

It does not really matter if is has a horn or not although some will argue that the horn prevents a rider from moving close to the horse along the crest of the neck during a jump. The Aussie saddle does provide an ample number of rings for saddle bags and other carried enclosures.

The saddle needs to fit the back of the horse or mule and distribute weight evenly along its back. If the withers are high and the gullet of the saddle presses against the withers or spine, this may cause problems with the horse and could result in nerve damage and cripple the horse.

The Aussie saddle needs a breastplate to prevent the saddle from sliding backward on the horse. A crupper is optional that keeps the saddle from sliding forward but this is usually needed only when the withers are less pronounced.

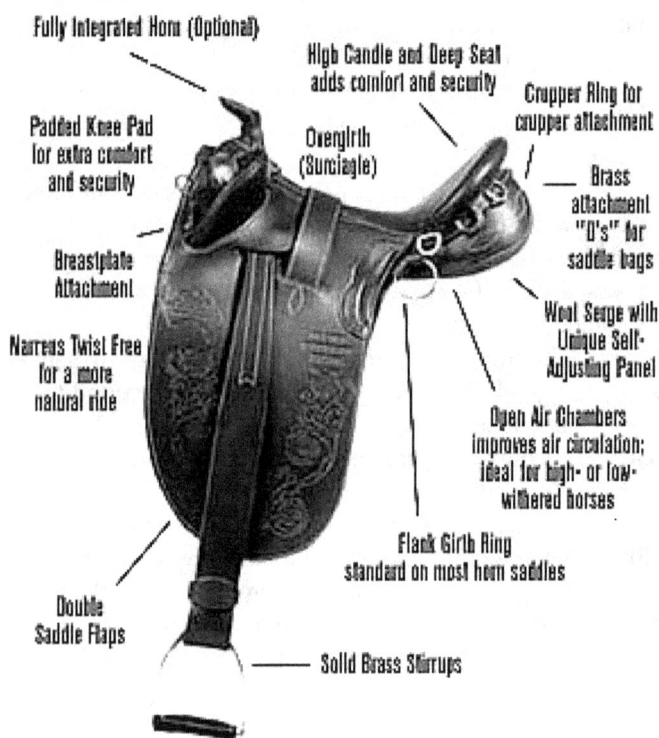

Fully Integrated Horn (Optional)

High Candle and Deep Seat adds comfort and security

Crupper Ring for crupper attachment

Padded Knee Pad for extra comfort and security

Overgirth (Surcingle)

Brass attachment "D's" for saddle bags

Breastplate Attachment

Narrows Twist Free for a more natural ride

Wool Serge with Unique Self-Adjusting Panel

Open Air Chambers improves air circulation; ideal for high- or low-withered horses

Flank Girth Ring standard on most horn saddles

Double Saddle Flaps

Solid Brass Stirrups

Saddlebags

It is recommended to carry two sets of double saddle bags. One set should be attached behind the saddle and the other set forward of the saddle. On top of the saddlebags in the back may be placed a bedroll, rain coat (slicker) and a tent tarp. Additional carry enclosures may include a gun scabbard, water canister case, ammunition bags and waterproof book/map bag. They should be made of leather or heavy waterproof canvas to assure long life use.

Choosing a Horse

The best way to know the ride of a horse is to ride the horse. However, there are a number of points of confirmation that should be considered in choosing a good military horse or mule for a Knight.

The temperament of the horse or mule must also be considered when choosing a mount for battle.

They need to be bold in spirit and not given to fear.

They need to bond with you as their sole master and trust you with their lives. They need to want to learn and be easily trained.

Points of Confirmation

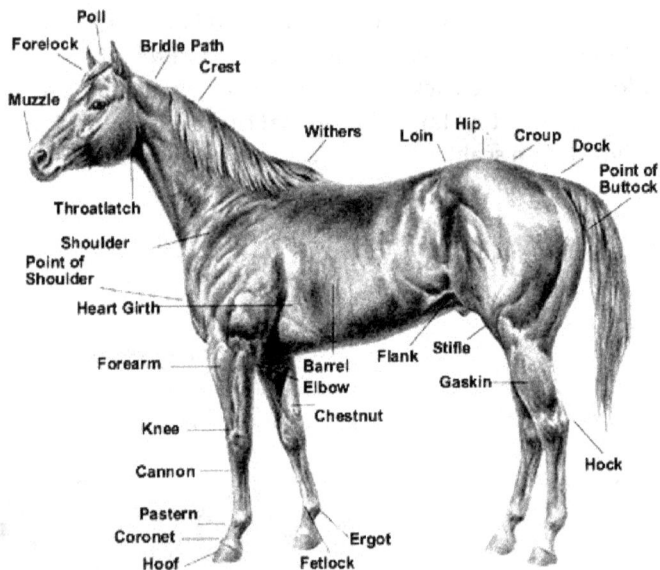

Poll, Forelock, Bridle Path, Crest, Muzzle, Withers, Loin, Hip, Croup, Dock, Point of Buttock, Throatlatch, Shoulder, Point of Shoulder, Heart Girth, Forearm, Flank, Stifle, Barrel, Elbow, Gaskin, Chestnut, Knee, Cannon, Hock, Pastern, Coronet, Ergot, Hoof, Fetlock

Balance

When evaluating a horse, the first thing to look for is balance. Does their neck, back and hip appear to be of equal length and be well proportioned? Does the horse's frame carry his muscle mass well? Too much muscle on a little frame or too little on a big one can result in problems.

Head

The eyes should be big and intelligent, not sunken or bulging and not too close together. The nostrils should be big to allow for serious air intake to fuel the body. Ears should be alert, pointing, and moving in all directions. Is the horse alert and aware of what's going on around him, does he appear in control and confident?

Side View

Feet - A horse's hooves must be able to withstand a great deal of pressure. Consider proportion, substance, and size of the hoof. The underside of the hoof should have a round, slightly oval shape with some depth. Some believe that larger feet indicate an aptitude for turf.

Pasterns - The pastern should be at a 45-degree angle. Its length should be proportionate - too long a pastern could indicate weakness and tendon strain, while if too short it may absorb too much concussion thus stressing the bone structure.

Ankle - As with the pastern, the ankle joint size should be proportionate to the rest of the leg.

Cannon Bones - Ideally, the cannon bone should be short, strong and have mass.

Knee - Bones in and leading to the knee should line up in a balanced manner - not tilting forward ("over at the knee") or back ("back at the knee").

Shoulder - The shoulder should have the same slope or angle as the pastern. Stride length is largely determined by the shoulder.

Neck - A horse's neck should be sufficient in scope so as to provide adequate wind for the horse, and be well tied in at the withers, while not being too low or "ewe necked". In short, does the neck fit the rest of the body?

Head - Nostrils should be of adequate size. The head should be broad enough to permit adequate air passage. Generally, the distance from the back of the jaw to where the head ties into the neck should be about the size of a fist.

Eyes - The eyes should be big and bright. Look for an "intelligent," keen, alert eye.

Back - The distance from the withers to top of croup or hips should match the length of the horse's neck from the poll to the withers.

Hip/Buttocks - The croup or hip should have a gentle slope - not too steep or flat. The gaskin should depict strength.

Hocks - A horse's hocks should not be straight as a post, nor curved so deeply as to be sickle hocked, or behind the body like a German Shepherd Dog. The horse should be standing balanced and straight.

Front View

Feet - Look for balanced feet on both sides and symmetry. Avoid misshapen, dished, or cracked feet.

Cannon Bones - From the front, the cannon bones should appear straight and of the same length.

Knees - It is best if the knees are set squarely on the top of the cannon bones, not off to one side or another - "offset knees."

Chest - A horse's chest should be broad, and appear powerful. Narrow chests or slab-sided horses are said to lack power.

Shoulder - Look for balance and symmetry.

Rear View

Hocks - From the rear, the hocks should appear to point straight at you, and not turn in or out -- "cow hocks."

Hip/Buttocks - Note that much of the animal's athleticism and power comes from behind.

Movement

Front/Rear view - The horse should move straight toward and away from you.

Observe whether the horse toes-in or toes-out as it walks.

Side view - Check for the overstep, meaning do the hind feet reach beyond the front hoof prints? Observe the horse's head. Be certain it does not bob unusually when walking as this may indicate soreness or lameness.

Walk - Look for a smooth long stride.

Feeding the Horse

The issue of feeding the horse is critical to their survival and thus the survival of the knight. The choice and quality of feed depends on the breeding and the raised environment of the horse.

A horse should be chosen who can survive easily on grass and a quart (10 lbs) of quality grain per day while also working in traveling 20 miles a day. Mules can travel farther on less food so are preferred for some missions.

This can be tested by working the horse over a two week period and feeding the horse 1 quart of grain per day and observe if the horse retains its muscle mass and energy.

Water should be provided no less than twice a day if possible. The horse should not drink or eat right after working but needs to cool down first. To not do this may result in colic in the digestive track of the horse.

Training the Horse

There are two levels of training required for the horse. First the horse is to be trained with a single rider and then once responsive to the rider in all skills, should be trained as a ride or in a group with quadrille maneuvers.

The horse should be trained in the aids to include the riders legs, position of seat, forward or backward weight shifting and by the hands through the reins. These are largely associated with dressage aids in communicating with the horse where little movement is seen by onlookers in the movement watching the rider communicate with his horse or mule.

The horse needs to be additionally trained in turning by the reins to include and two-hand reining and neck reining. Training also includes the natural progression of movement from the stand through walk, trot, cantor and gallop; a change of lead; extending and compressing the trot and in jumping.

Turning on the forehand and the haunches along with side stepping should also be mastered by the horse and rider.

When the above is achieved, the horse and rider may join the quadrille teams and learn the unified parade movements with others in rides of 2, 4, 8, and 12 riders. These skills should be learned both by command on the fly and as a choreographed ride.

It is optional for each Commandery to choose the custom and style of commands. My training is with the British Horse Society so I use their command terminology for dressage and quadrilles exclusively.

Working the Horse

There is extensive history found in various horse cavalry manuals as to what should be expected of a horse when grouped with hundreds of other horses. Generally, a good horse should be provided the following schedule when at work.

- A horse should not be worked at the trot more than 20 minutes at a time and then be given 10 minutes at the walk to cool off. If it is a forced march, 20 minutes trot, 10 minutes walk and return to trot for 20 minutes can be held for many hours.
- The horse and rider should be given 10 minutes break every hour to stop and rest if they are expected to reach their destination with any energy left to engage the enemy.
- A day of work should be 8-10 hours with an average distance of travel being 20-30 miles per day.

- At each hour break, the rider should recheck the saddle and tack to assure it is not causing discomfort to the horse. The cinch may be loosened and the horse allowed its head to feed off of the natural grasses in the area during the break.

Shoeing the Horse

The need for shoes for a horse depends on the kind of terrain where the horse and rider find themselves . If a horse is in the sand or soft dirt, the horse may not need to be shod or perhaps just the front hooves shod. However, if the terrain causes the wearing away of the hoof, then shoes will be needed.

It is recommend that every knight be able to replace a shoe on his horse in an emergency. To be able to do this, a knight should minimally carry a shoeing hammer, nails and a small hoof file. A hammer-hachet would also work as a dual purpose tool.

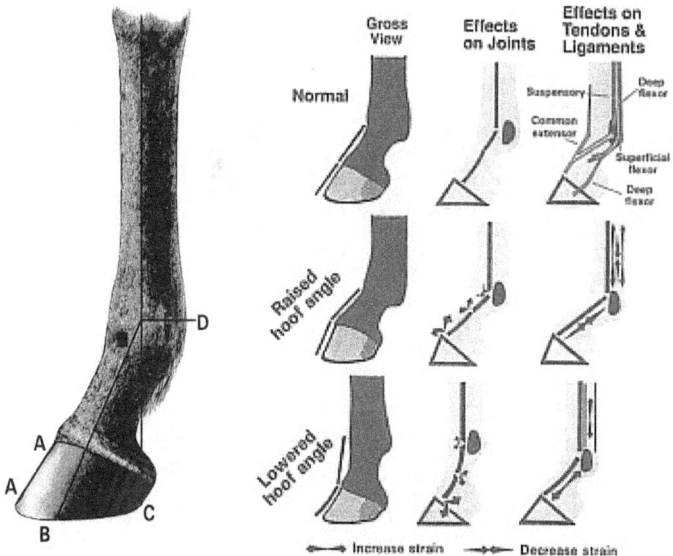

In the figure above, we observe the relative position of the hoof in relationship to the rest of the limb. Line B represents the "angle of incidence" defined by the axes of the phalangeal bones.

Line C bisects the metacarpus (metatarsus) and extends distally to brush the palmar (plantar) border of the heels on the ground surface of the wall. (illustration adapted from Russell, W. 1903)

A well shod horse provides a good support from the shoe evenly around the horn of the hoof and lifts the frog from riding along the ground and wearing down.

In addition, the nails should be placed well into the horn to assure a solid fit while not penetrating into the live tissue of the hoof. Nails should be cinched up by the hammer using the file as a clincher to assure a tight fit.

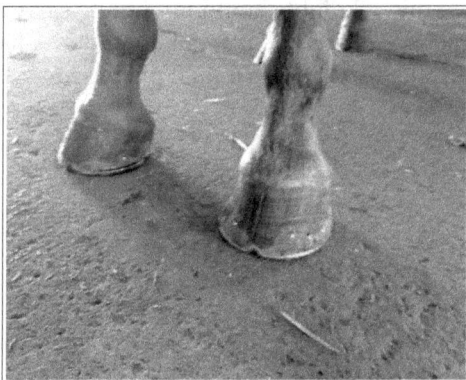

The balance of the hoof needs to be flat on the ground with an even line from the hoof up through the canon bone as viewed from the front. From the side it should be in line with the natural angle of the canon bone.

A poorly shod horse will not last when going many miles and in battle. As they say "for the loss of a shoe I lost my horse and for the loss of the horse I lost the war."

13. Communications
Short Wave Radio

Communications between the knights when deployed in the field is vital to a combined effort should this become needed. It is advised that older more robust technologies be employed with the addition of modern encryption capabilities. This choice is to avoid the destructive result of EMP.

The best platform for communications is still the short wave radio (HAM) with an encryption and decryption capability. This means a small device will be needed which can be interfaced with the radio to provide encryption capability. This does not need to be digital encryption protocol but could be an analog system.

Hand Held Radios

Since engagement with the enemy may be in the mountains, a 30 mile short wave system is minimally recommended for each knight. Any larger than this in power and distance and it becomes cumbersome in size and excessive in its power needs. Smaller hand held 5-watt short wave radios are usually limited to a 5-10 mile radius and may be the best solution in some cases.

It may be we return to a Morse code type approach that is spread spectrum and ground transmitted using Tesla technologies.

Licensing is currently required by the FCC to use these radios and they are limited by law to non-commercial use. However, as the economy crashes and the US becomes completely over taken by the NWO, such restrictions will no longer be considered important.

Base Radios

In addition to every knight having a hand held radio, base radios will be deployed wherever offensive bases are located.

These radios will be high powered and can transmit for hundreds of miles. Antennas should be hidden in trees and be powered by solar or wind whenever possible. The base transceivers are to be located in underground command bases where a substantial amount of earth mass will keep the base from being easily discovered by sensor devices. However, this will not hide the transmission from radio directional sensors.

Compact Crystal Receivers

As a complement to these base radios, a very low cost crystal set receiver will be developed in mass and given or sold to local supporting residents as a warning and informational radio broadcast network. This network will be activated when all other FCC commercial stations are commandeered and controlled by the misinformation wing of the NWO.

These crystal receiver sets should cost less than $3.00 each and may be sent out as a kit in a mass mailing to residents in an area or available through other supporting organizations.

Knights will also have these passive receiver sets to receive command directives so they do not have to use their short wave transceivers which can provide a radio signature to the enemy in compromising their location.

Line of Sight Antennas

There is a certain design of antenna that is a largely a line of site antenna. This is being researched. Communications using the short wave signal can be transmitted through such a narrow beam antenna to reduce the possibility of the enemy outside of this line of sight corridor from intercepting the signal.

Alternative Communications

It is well known that light based communications cannot be compromised unless the line of sight is known and is tapped to intercept the communications. Any radio frequency can be transduced into a light signal 'beam' for transmission. Simplified communications as mentioned above may include a modified Morse code using a reflective mirror or even smoke signals in very remote areas.

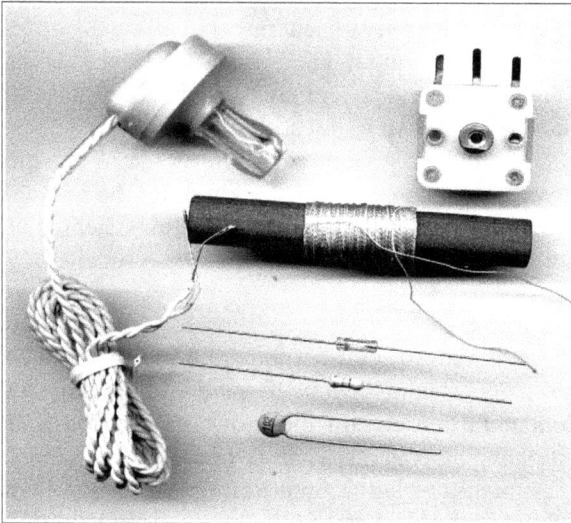

Simple Crystal Receiver Radio

14. Wilderness Survival

Human Needs

The art of survival in the wilderness is more challenging in a cold winter verses a summer camp environment in the forest. Generally, sheltering against the elements, food, heat for warmth and cooking and, water are vital requirements for survival. A silent weapon for hunting is needed in addition to the ability to make traps for catching small game. Guns are noisy revealing location and are used as a last resort in all cases.

The following devices can be adapted to be carried on a bike or horse. The tent poles can be found locally or a break-down pole can be substituted.

In the Rocky Mountains, winter temps can drop below minus 40 degrees and quickly drain the human and animal body of heat. At these temperatures, heat is absolutely necessary for human and horse survival.

Shelter and Heat

If making a semi-permanent camp that will be used for weeks, take the time to assure it blocks the wind, shelters you from the rain and snow and provides a means of heat using natural resources (wood) <u>within</u> the shelter. The design of the Native American tipi still is a superior design using the least amount of materials with a fire inside as a heat source.

The tipi frame wood can be found in most forests so all that is needed is to carry is a waterproof and fire resistant tarp of the right cut for a tipi.

The Rocket Stove design seems to be the most portable... carried by bike or by horse.

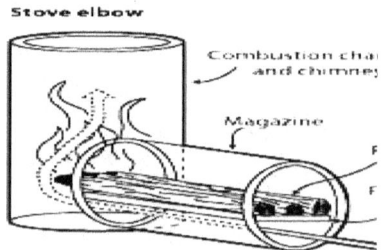

Winiarski / Aprovecho rocket stove

Stove elbow

Combustion cha and chimne

Magazine

PLAINS INDIAN TEPEE

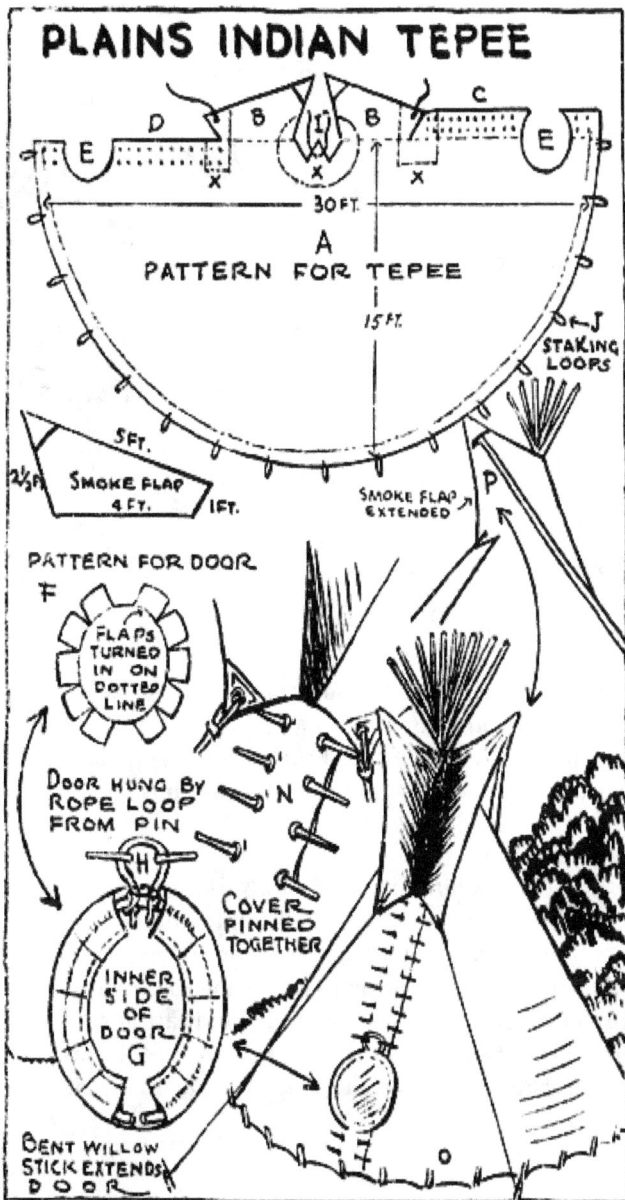

D B B C

E E

X X X

← 30 FT. →

A

PATTERN FOR TEPEE

15 FT.

↖ J
STAKING
LOOPS

5 FT.

2⅓ FT. SMOKE FLAP
4 FT. 1 FT.

SMOKE FLAP
EXTENDED

P

PATTERN FOR DOOR

F

FLAPS
TURNED
IN ON
DOTTED
LINE

DOOR HUNG BY
ROPE LOOP
FROM PIN

H

N

COVER
PINNED
TOGETHER

INNER
SIDE
OF
DOOR
G

BENT WILLOW
STICK EXTENDS
DOOR

O

This teepee design is to be preferred over many conventional tents in that it can have the heat source inside the Tipi rather then outside where the heat is largely lost.

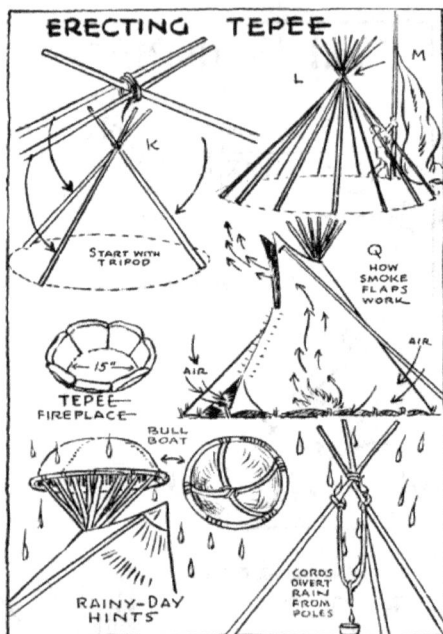

ERECTING TEPEE

START WITH TRIPOD

HOW SMOKE FLAPS WORK

TEPEE FIREPLACE

BULL BOAT

RAINY-DAY HINTS

CORDS DIVERT RAIN FROM POLES

Hunting Food

It is expected that a knight will have a weapon to hunt for food as needed. It should be a silent weapon so as not to be heard. The simple bow and arrow is the easiest projectile weapon to make in an emergency and it promises acceptable accuracy. I personally carry a small crossbow.

Making a Bow

As an alternative to the bow, one can choose breakdown crossbows and small compound bows that can be broken down into smaller parts for carrying inside of a tent tarp or slicker. For small game, the 80 pound pistol crossbows are adequate for hunting and can store in a very compact space. The bolts at the time of this writing are about $0.30 each which is cheaper than many rifle rounds.

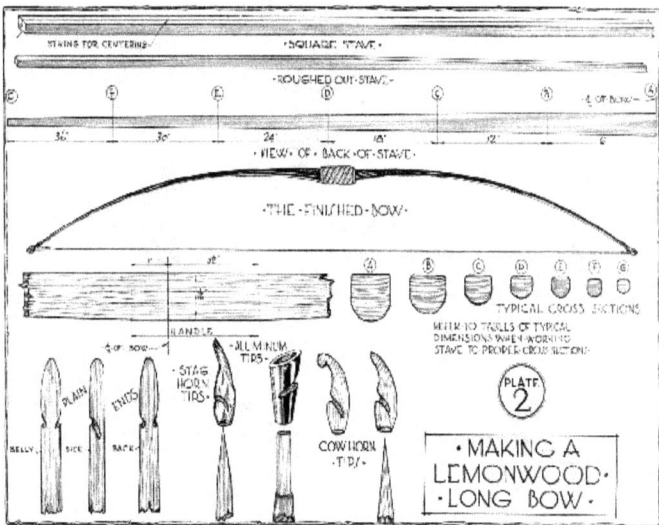

Plate 2: MAKING A LEMONWOOD LONG BOW

Snares

In addition to the use of the bow for hunting, the use of wire snares for catching game is recommended. A wire snare should not be left for long periods of time and a bell or rattle may be added to the snare so when it is triggered by an animal, it is heard and the hunter can go to the site and kill the game so it does not suffer.

There are many snare designs. It is advised that the knight has these already made and included as a part of his kit for living and surviving in the woods.

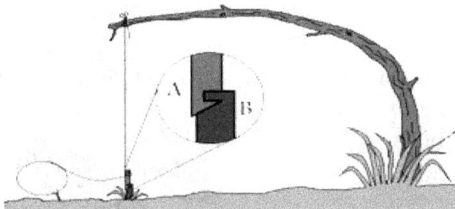

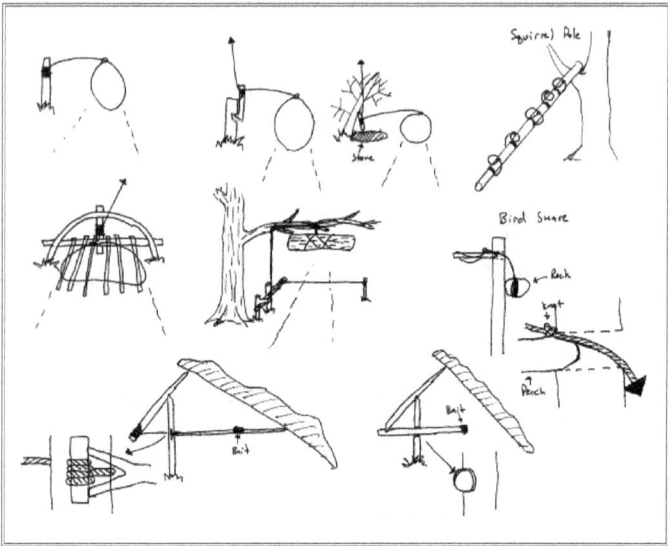

Water

Water is best when drawn from a rolling mountain stream not far from its source. Springs are commonly found in the mountains and are an excellent source of potable water.

Filtering Water

If you are not sure of the quality of the water, it should be boiled or water purifier pills may be added. If the knight has a small water filter that is designed to remove all pathogens and toxins, this may be used instead of boiling or purifying pills.

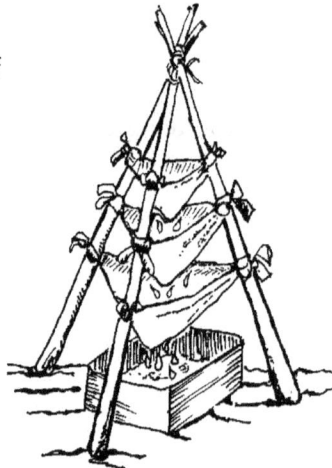

If none of these are available, you can make a useful water filter from the charcoal left over from your fire with sand and gravel layers. The top layer of the three part filter can be grass and small stones to get out the larger particulates. The second layer is fine sand and the bottom layer is a bountiful amount of small bits of charcoal. Any material can be used for making the layers such as bandannas or even plastic with a hole in the bottom.

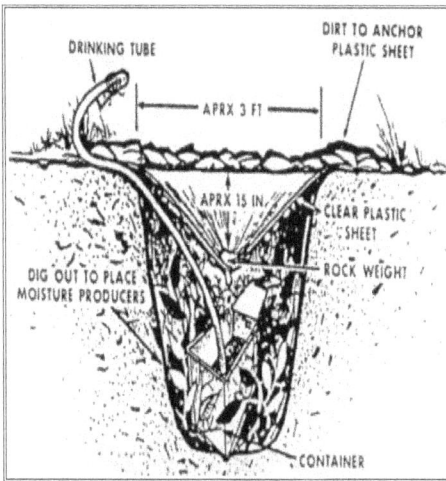

Dry Land Water

In the case where it is a dry climate and no springs or streams are to be found in the area, dew condensation is an optional source from which to gather water for man and animal.

The system above will gather water when there is sufficient sunshine to heat up the system and available moist green vegetation that holds a sufficient amount of water. As the bruised vegetation heats up, it causes its moisture to evaporate and rises to be collected by the plastic. It then drips into a container placed in the bottom of the hole.

A drinking tube may be used to retrieve the water or if this is not available, the container may be retrieved with the water then poured into canteen for future use.

Making Fire

If you cannot keep warm with clothing and sleeping gear in a cold camp, you must make a fire. Every knight and soldier should carry a fire starter that may be magnesium bar with a striker. These cost but a few dollars and are a life saver when cold. If these are not available, a fire can be made using friction if you can find dry tinder.

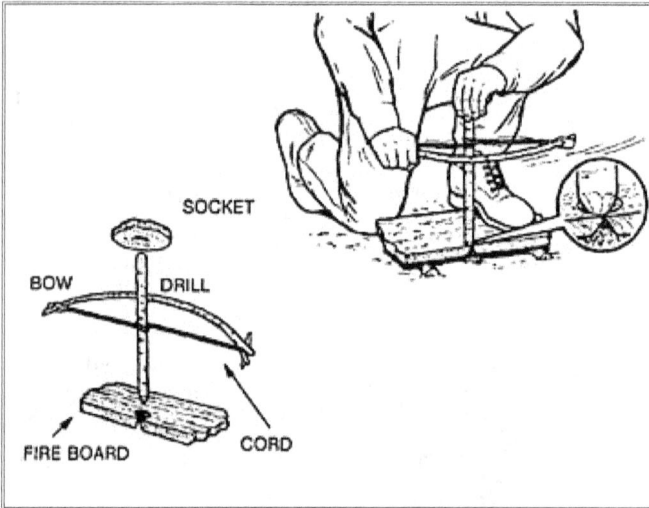

Taking the time to make a bow and finding the best tinder will save you when cold. Tinder may be dried moss, shredded dry bark wood, a piece of loose weave cloth or other fine material.

Tinder needs to be very dry and combustible and easy to light with just a red glow ember with the process done out of the wind.

I would recommend having a number of fire starting solutions including wax coated matches and even a lighter. Better more than less when your survival is at stake in a cold environment.

15. First Aid

There are many books out on first aid including those from the Red Cross. Our concern here is for Emergency First Aid to save the life of a member or friend of the Order.

It is required that every individual within the Order of the Gate in the field has with them an emergency first aid kit with a booklet that covers many of the most common ailments and injuries.

Minimally, medical instructions must cover stopping severe blood loss, mending broken bones, snake bites, and treating severely bruised or torn muscles and ligaments. In the case of severe cut wounds, it should instruct in treating for infection and in sewing up the wound. Superglue is now commonly used for closing wounds. The kit may also include the procedure for probing and removing bullets. The kit must provide the needed instructions and instruments that would be needed to complete all of the life-saving medical procedures.

There are many natural remedies that may be found in the field and these should be identified and collected if possible by knowledgeably medical personnel for later use on man and horse. Such remedies may be used in treating headaches, stomach issues, fatigue, infections and other physical ailments.

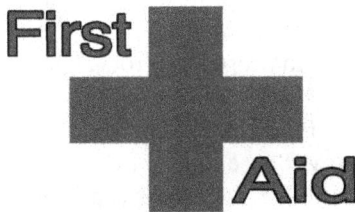

16. Mounted Training Exercises

Whether riding a bike or horse, training to ride in good form is necessary. For the horse, discipline of both horse and rider is a must and all diligence should be directed at assuring they are both properly trained for stealth in battle. In the preferred model, it may be as few as one or two in a team who are deployed on a mission. In some circumstances, the primary mode of transport will be the horse since it creates the least identifiable signature on enemy sensor systems.

The horse needs to be trained to the leg, seat and hand aids of the rider. The horse needs to be motionless until the rider gives it an aid to perform an activity. The horse needs to be trained to be silent and calm even in the midst of threat and noise. The aids given by the rider need to be near motionless so as to not give away position by movement.

The best means of providing this training is first as a single rider and then in the manage' or arena in teams or rides of 2, 4, 8 and 12 members. The principles of dressage originated from cavalry training and this becomes the method of training that we use in the Orders.

My preference is the dressage training method of the British Horse Society. In all cases, there is a 'preparatory command' that prepares the horse and rider for the next change in activity and then the 'execute command' that gives the activity its start. Commands may include the following forms:

Company to halt.... halt!
Left column prepare to trot.... column trot
Ride in twos left alternate right turn.... left turn!...
         right turn!..... etc.
Company form a line..... Right turn!

More of these commands can be found in the BHS approved instructors book for riding in the manage' or arena.

17. Starting a Commandery

Members of a Commandery (Chapter)

The Commandery or chapter is a group of knights working together on a mission at a field location or base. It is fulfilling a mission given to it by the Abbot General or a Commander and riders are always considered to be deployed in enemy territory 'behind the lines'.

Generally up to 12 knights with their support units may be attached to a Commandery. This is potentially about 60 - 80 men including the Knights, Sergeants, Soldiers and Chaplains.

Knight Commander

One knight will be elected and then approved by the Abbot General from among the body of knights to become the Knight Commander for the Commandery. It will be a man who is a natural leader, skilled and fearless in battle and is looked up to by the rest of the Knights as a man of honor and virtue. He will be chosen after recommendations are given to the Abbot General by the other Knights who would serve under the command of the new Knight Commander.

Officer Posts

Within the Commandery, there are a number of officer posts that will be held by the Knights under the Knight Commander. The Command Staff posts include but are not limited to:

1. Executive Officer (2nd in Command)
2. Animal Officer: In charge of assessing the condition of the horses (and other animals) and treating for ailments.
3. Training Officer: In charge of field training of horse and rider in the stealth modality.

4. Weapons Officer: In charge of weapons acquisition, marksman training and ammunition supplies.

5. Communications Officer: In charge of communications radios and communications training.

6. Intelligence Officer: In charge of receiving all intelligence information and providing an analysis of the data to make life-saving decisions.

7. Medical Officer: In charge of medical emergencies, first aid training and assuring medical kits are stocked.

8. Logistics Officer: In charge of securing supplies and horse and rider transportation.

9. Chaplain: In charge of morale and moral leadership. He will not likely be a knight but a priest of the of the Order of the Culdee. However, he would hold the status of a knight in rank but without a command.

Starting a Commandery

For a Commandery to be recognized, at least three knights of the Order of the Gate need to be engaged in a long-term mission at a specific location and petition the Abbot General to establish a Commandery. Upon approval, the Abbot General will issue a letter of Charter establishing a Commandery within the Order of the Gate. In the Charter, it will issue a Charter number and Charter name for the Commandery . It may be revocable by the Abbot General at any time.

Locations for a Commandery

The location for a Commandery will include many locations in the US and overseas.

In the US, it is the desire of the Abbot General to have Commanderies established at the marked locations on the following map which are considered to be safe places after the coming collapse of the US economy and the man-activated ravage of natural disasters. There are other places not on the following map as determined safe by the prophets of the Order.

It is recommended that Commanderies be located close to Native American Reserves or adverse terrain whenever possible that can only be maneuvered by horse or mule.

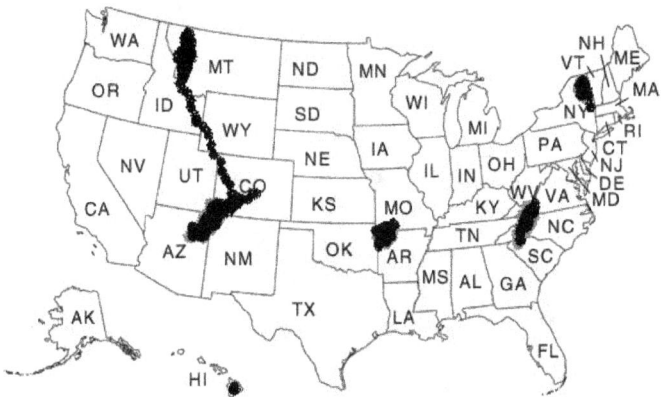

Commanderies overseas in Europe will be primarily established within the still existing Kingdoms of the Holy Roman Empire to include Britain, France, Germany, Switzerland, Portugal, Spain and Italy. These are chosen because we have the consent by Lynda Von Habsburg who is the Empress of the Holy Roman Empire to have a presence in these countries.

Commanderies in the Middle East would initially include North Israel near the ancient city of Acre is located on the plain of Megeddo (aka: Valley of Armageddon), Jerusalem and West Jordan near the ruins of ancient Petra and Syria.

It may also include the Persian Gulf such as in Gatar and Bahrain. I say this because recently I have been shown that Syria will become a hot spot in world domination with 1000 Caliphs rising up against the NWO in battle.

18. Mobile Commandery

One of the approved models of the Orders is the Commandery in riding motorcycles as a Mobile Commandery. The objective is to spread the word about the existence of the Order to seek out and recruit future Knights, Sergeants, Soldiers and Chaplains for the Order. It would also be commissioned to assist the needy, the disadvantaged and the oppressed as they encounter them in their travels. Biker rallies and related events will be the primary target for attendance.

A Mobile Commandery is structured the same way as a Base Commandery. The minimum number of knights required for establishing a Mobile Commandery is three knights with their supporting units. Rank and protocol is to be followed.

The preferred motorcycle is a Harley or other larger bike that is sufficiently powered to ride comfortably on the highways of America. It should be dressed out with sufficient dry storage for long distance travel with the gear needed to camp-out comfortably in any adverse weather.

State law needs to be considered in the choice of weapons that may be carried. When the NWO finally suspends the US Constitution in denying the right to bear arms for Americans, this concern will no longer be important. We will continue to embrace and protect all of our inalienable rights as Americans.

The uniform for the Mobile Commandery may conform to the black leathers common to biker clubs with an approved 'patch' centered on the coat or vest of each member.

New recruits will be attached to a knight for training and follow the standard promotion sequence beginning as a Soldier.

19. Dream-Vision: 7th Legion

The Dream

In the early morning of the 21st of September 2016, I had a dream of civil war that encompassed the earth. One did not know who was their friend and who was the enemy.
Soldier fighting soldier of the same uniform was common. If they shot at you, you shot back.

The dream began back in the time of Rome in perhaps the 2nd century in Iberia (Spain) also called Hispania. In the dream, a friend and I were generals in this former legion.

Underground Armies

I was then shown a vast underground world that was the home to the 7th Legion. I remember the green rolling hills of the

area in a mountainous region somewhere in the world where the 7th Legion had its base. Each time the 7th Legion was needed, they emerged from a horizontal seam or low overhang in the rocks just at a man's height as a full vast army marching in military order from the earth.

I then understood this army were made up of Celtiberians or Celts, Hebrews and other people groups living formerly in what today is Spain/France.

Wars Over Time

In the 2nd century, we seemed to be somewhere in the East. Then we were brought forward in time into perhaps the 4th century in Western Europe and again in the 8th century in America. My friend and I again fought and led the 7th Legion army during a time of vast civil war in today's modern times.

As the scene unfolded in modern times, I was holding an assault rifle that was the envy of others. I looked to my friend and we spoke out and agreed;

"It is time for for the 7th Legion to rise again."

Men then started to gather around us and became this 7th legion as we marched into battle in what seemed to be SW America. There were many battles in the wide open spaces, the mountains and also battles were fought in the cities.

The dream then ended.

Interpretation

As I was awake, I knew there was something special about the 7th Legion of the Roman Army. After research I discovered the following.

The 7th Legion consisted of about 7000 men. It was founded in Spain and took part in the conquering of

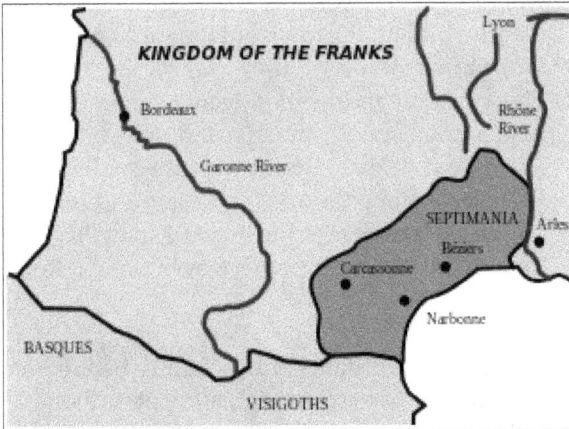

Gaul under the reign of Julius Cesar in 74 BC. It was primarily stationed in NE Spain into the 4th century but did campaigns into Germany, Britain, North Africa and other areas of Europe and Asia. On many occasions, it was used to fight a civil war within the Roman Empire.

Septimania

The old surname of the 7th Legion, **Paterna** can be translated as "the old one." Veteran soldiers of the Seventh are believed to have settled in Septimania which was during this time a Hebrew State consisting of the exiles from Israel migrating there up until circa 140 CE. The 7th legion settled among them.

The Seventh legion, however, has a more direct link to Nimes. Why? Because veteran soldiers of the Seventh are believed to have settled in Septimania. Another possible derivation of the towns name is the reference to the seven cities of the same territory: Béziers, Elne, Agde, Narbonne, Lodève, Maguelonne and Nîmes.

When Delmas writes "One was established at Nimes, which was drawn from the legion which went to Egypt to conquer Mark Antony, and because of that, the town of Nimes has a crocodile for its arms"

This probably means the Seventh legion too, which colonized Septimania and two of its cities, Nimes and Beziers. Presumably the soldiers, for Delmas, farming the land at Beziers and Nimes also decided to live at the thermal spa village of Rennes-les-Bains. Or perhaps even build a Roman Bath there?

It is thought the name of the country Septimania comes from the number seven (sept) and got its name from the Roman 7th Legion Veterans who settled there.

The name "Septimania" may derive from part of the Roman name of the city of Béziers, Colonia Julia Septimanorum Beaterrae, which in turn alludes to the settlement of veterans of the Roman VII Legion in the city. Another possible derivation of the name is in reference to the seven cities (civitates) of the territory: Béziers, Elne, Agde, Narbonne, Lodève, Maguelonne, and Nîmes.

Septimania extended to a line halfway between the Mediterranean and the Garonne River in the northwest; in the east the Rhône separated it from Provence; and to the south its boundary was formed by the Pyrenees. (Wikipedia)

Calalus in America

Septimania is the key here in the dream. It is believed it was the settling veterans of the 7th Legion within Septimania that provided the military discipline and training for what became the army of the Kingdom of Calalus in America circa 775 to 1000 CE in the South West region or the lower four corners area of the United States.

By 719, the Muslim Arabs had invaded Septimania thus dispersing the existing armies of Septimania with the Capital Nabonne not retaken from the Muslims until 759 CE.

About this time, Charlemagne granted Emperor status by the Roman Church came to power. He was tolerant with the Israelite State of Septimania, yet some appeared to leave the area at this time in escaping Charlemagne's control and that of the Holy Roman Empire that Charlemagne led. Where did these Sons of the 7th Legion go one might ask? To America is the most reasonable answer.

Structure of the Legion

The rank structure of the Roman Legion by the 2nd century was still based on foot soldiers as their primary force. However in battle with the Germanic tribes, this failed as the
German cavalry often overran the foot solders. By the 6th century, the Roman Legion divided into a full cavalry and a full infantry under separate commanders at the Tribune level of command.

The numbers below do not reflect the non-fighting support staff to include blacksmiths, cooks, and other logistical trades. The Roman rank system is as follows:

GROUP	LED BY	NUMBER	EQUAVA LENT	LED BY	COUNT
Contuber nium	Decanus	8 men (tent buddies)	Squad	Sergeant	10 Contuber nium= Centuriu m
Centuriu m	Centurian	80 men	Platoon/T roop	Comman der	5-6 Centuriu m = Cohort
Cohort	Tribune Legate	480 men	Company	Captain	10 Cohorts = Legion
Legion	Legate	4800 men + 120 horsemen	Brigade	General	

By the 6th century, possibly 20-50 percent of the Legion were mounted cavalry enabling the legion to move more quickly in varied fields of battle and terrain. The mounted cavalry was fully armored and often carried a small shield, bow, spear, shorter lance tipped with a 10" blade and, a sword.

The core unit of this army is the Centurium (80 men) built from 10 squads of 8 men who are a tightly trained team. The US Military still embraces the ancient Squad

unit size with some extending the squad number from 8 to 12 men.

Borders of the Kingdom

The Kings of Calalus were many as identified on the Tuscan Artifacts all with Hebrew names. They wrote on these artifacts that they ruled over the Toltecs and finally lost to them in war in circa 1000 CE.

Their land in the SW began at the Rio Grand stretching through Los Lunas, NM and seemed to span to Phoenix in the NW where they found the Santa Cruz River and spread south to Tuscan.

They seemed to finally inhabit the waterways connected to the Gila River to the south and moving east along the Gila River toward the Gila Mountains in New Mexico. They seemed to settle along the the Santa Cruz and San Pedro rivers and other tributaries and streams that all dumped into the Gila River to the North.

Army to Rise Again

The notion that it is time for this army to rise again is appropriate in supporting and protecting the mission and people of YHWH reflected in the mission of Septimania and now Calalus in America. It can be reasoned that it was the sons of the original 7th Legion that became the armies of the Kingdom of Calalus in America for which Roman military relics were discovered in 1924 called the Tuscan Artifacts dating to circa 750 CE. It is highly probable that the 7th Legion was made of of Hebrews in Exile from its founding.

These artifacts with Latin, Greek and Hebrew script indicate the people of Calalus were a fusion of Christian, Celtic, Hebrew and Roman in culture.

Possible Spiritual Army

It is believed by some that this Kingdom of Calalus will rise again in the legacy of the 7th Legion to preserve the liberties of the faithful of YHWH who keep the Sabbath blessings (Saturday Sabbath).

I must admit it may not be a literal army that is raised up at all but the righteous souls from the 7th Legion down through history who have died who will then request to return as a 'spiritual' advance army Brigade sent early from the vast armies of Y'Shua prior to his coming.

It also could be a very real army or even both kinds of armies. This may be the meaning of the armies emerging from underground - a hidden place since they are not physical but spiritual beings who will be fighting along side the angels of YHWH before the return of Y'Shua.

Update 11/15/2016

In prayer today, I was reminded of the great army raised up from dry bones by YHWH as prophesied by Ezekiel that would be raised up in these end times.

I was shown this included the army of the 7th legion of this dream with the resurrection of the Israelite armies of Calalus who had once ruled in America circa 750 to 1000 AD. This army also includes the living genetic Israelites who have forgotten their roots. The massive army would in time make its way to Israel as the true Israelites of Judah and Jacob/Ephraim in repossessing their homeland of Israel.

Ezekiel 37 King James Version (KJV)

1 The hand of the Lord was upon me, and carried me out in the spirit of the Lord, and set me down in the midst of the valley which was full of bones, 2 And caused me to pass by them round about: and, behold, there were very many in the open valley; and, lo, they were very dry.

3 And he said unto me, Son of man, can these bones live? And I answered, O Lord God, thou knowest.

4 Again he said unto me, Prophesy upon these bones, and say unto them, O ye dry bones, hear the word of the Lord.

5 Thus saith the Lord God unto these bones; Behold, I will cause breath to enter into you, and ye shall live:

6 And I will lay sinews upon you, and will bring up flesh upon you, and cover you with skin, and put breath in you, and ye shall live; and ye shall know that I am the Lord.

7 So I prophesied as I was commanded: and as I prophesied, there was a noise, and behold a shaking, and the bones came together, bone to his bone.

8 And when I beheld, lo, the sinews and the flesh came up upon them, and the skin covered them above: but there was no breath in them.

9 Then said he unto me, Prophesy unto the wind, prophesy, son of man, and say to the wind, Thus saith the Lord God; Come from the four winds, O breath, and breathe upon these slain, that they may live.

10 So I prophesied as he commanded me, and the breath came into them, and they lived, and stood up upon their feet, an exceeding great army.

11 Then he said unto me, Son of man, these bones are the whole house of Israel: behold, they say, Our bones are dried, and our hope is lost: we are cut off for our parts.

12 Therefore prophesy and say unto them, Thus saith the Lord God; Behold, O my people, I will open your graves, and cause you to come up out of your graves, and bring you into the land of Israel.

13 And ye shall know that I am the Lord, when I have opened your graves, O my people, and brought you up out of your graves,

14 And shall put my spirit in you, and ye shall live, and I shall place you in your own land: then shall ye know that I the Lord have spoken it, and performed it, saith the Lord.

15 The word of the Lord came again unto me, saying,

16 Moreover, thou son of man, take thee one stick, and write upon it, For Judah, and for the children of Israel his companions: then take another stick, and write upon it, For Joseph, the stick of Ephraim and for all the house of Israel his companions:

17 And join them one to another into one stick; and they shall become one in thine hand.

18 And when the children of thy people shall speak unto thee, saying, Wilt thou not shew us what thou meanest by these?

19 Say unto them, Thus saith the Lord God; Behold, <u>I will take the stick of Joseph, which is in the hand of Ephraim, and the tribes of Israel his fellows, and will put them with him, even with the stick of Judah, and make them one stick, and they shall be one in mine hand.</u>

20 And the sticks whereon thou writest shall be in thine hand before their eyes.

21 And say unto them, Thus saith the Lord God; Behold, <u>I will take the children of Israel from among the heathen, whither they be gone, and will gather them on every side, and bring them into their own land:</u>

22 And I will make them one nation in the land upon the mountains of Israel; and one king shall be king to them all: and they shall be no more two nations, neither shall they be divided into two kingdoms any more at all.

23 Neither shall they defile themselves any more with their idols, nor with their detestable things, nor with any of their transgressions: but I will save them out of all their dwelling places, wherein they have sinned, and will cleanse them: so shall they be my people, and I will be their God.
24 And David my servant shall be king over them; and they all shall have one shepherd: they shall also walk in my judgments, and observe my statutes, and do them.
25 And they shall dwell in the land that I have given unto Jacob my servant, wherein your fathers have dwelt; and they shall dwell therein, even they, and their children, and their children's children for ever: and my servant David shall be their prince for ever.
26 Moreover I will make a covenant of peace with them; it shall be an everlasting covenant with them: and I will place them, and multiply them, and will set my sanctuary in the midst of them for evermore.
27 My tabernacle also shall be with them: yea, I will be their God, and they shall be my people.
28 And the heathen shall know that I the Lord do sanctify Israel, when my sanctuary shall be in the midst of them for evermore.

20. Sword of Goliath

The Dream-Vision

In the early morning of the 9th of June 2012, I had a dream where I found myself in a dense evergreen forest and as I was walking though a small clearing, I saw the hilt of a sword just emerging from the earth. I stopped and reached down and pulled the sword out of the dirt. As I was pulling out the sword, I heard an angel above and behind me say,

"The Sword of Goliath... to fight [kill] the Nephilim."

The sword was rusty and was not fit for battle until it was cleaned and sharpened. My task (as a blacksmith – which I am) was to prepare the sword for battle.

Battle Against the Nephilim

As I awoke, I realized the battle against the Nephilim was coming in great force and that the Church was not prepared for this kind of battle. Thus the sword was rusty and unsharpened. It had to be cleaned and sharpened which is the training of an army to be ready for this kind of battle in the spiritual and physical realm as the 3rd and 4th dimensions merge in these last days..

The necessity of the full Armor of God was also needed and must be rightly fitted to each warrior since the battle was first spiritual and then played out in the physical world. I believe the future battles will be very real with real swords and with real armies but only the pure in heart and the faithful will be victorious in battle. It is reality that such wars are first fought and won in the spiritual realm that will determine the outcome of who lives and dies in the physical realm.

King Arthur

History suggests that King Arthur of the Seed of the Kings of Israel also fought against the the Nephilim in Wales with the enemy described as 'giants'.

The sword he used was named Excalibur and some believe it was the actual sword of Goliath brought to Britannia by the royal line of the Queens of Avalon from the Hebrew State of Septimania in France circa the 3rd or 4th centuries.

The State of Septimania is known in history as founded by James, the royal brother of Jesus who represented the ruling line of King David after the resurrection and ascension of Jesus.

This line was carried into the line of Queen Vivian of Avalon, the mother of Gweniviere who married King Arthur. It is possible that it was from Queen Vivian that the sword Excalibur originated – the alleged sword of Goliath.

Cleansing the Holy Land

The shepherd David was the one chosen by God (YHWH) to lead the armies of Israel into battle against the Nephilim Goliath. King David reunited Israel and Judah and used the sword of Goliath to overcome the many forces of the Nephilim still residing in Canaan.

Apparently the land of Canaan was full of this hybrid species birthed from the fallen angels and the daughters of men. They needed to be cleansed from the earth as commanded by God (YHWH) in the book of Enoch.

This cleansing of the land would enable the seed of Adam to again rule the Holy Land being last ruled by the line of Melchizedek (Shem) as the Priest-King of Salem (Jerusalem) who blessed Abraham.

Third Crusade Fights the Nephilim and their Demons

The story to follow may be real (or may not??) but is acknowledged by the Templars of Britannia as more a history than a myth.

The Great Disjunction

In the year 1192, Richard the Lion heart, King of England, ventured across Europe during the Third Crusade. At the height of this aggression the fabric of

reality was briefly torn, allowing a short but devastating influx of magic and spirit-kind to be unleashed across the Earth.

When Saladin's forces failed to pay tribute demanded by the crusaders, Richard's trusted adviser whispered to his king that the Muslims should be punished and their threat ended for all time.

The adviser told Richard to gather several holy artifacts to the city so that a divine ritual could be initiated to bless Richard's forces and curse their foes. Believing his counsel, Richard unknowingly brought several powerful artifacts together -- and these artifacts, relics of creation itself, and of such power, began to undo reality simply through their congregation.

As the material fabric of Earth tore, spirit-kind and magic were unleashed across the world. Hordes of demons and strange beings of power sprung up in the streets of Acre, surrounding Richard's army.

After heavy losses, Richard and Saladin joined forces to wade through the hordes. With incredible valor, the two heroes wounded the adviser, now revealed to be a 'dark' magi of considerable power. The adviser fled, along with a host of the evil creatures, allowing Richard and Saladin to seal the breach.

Although the battle lasted but a few hours, the Disjunction, as it would come to be called, unleashed vast forces across the entire planet, changing history forever.

Realizing that the ritual could never be allowed to occur again, both Richard and Saladin swore to divide the relics and secure them in their respective lands. The Knights Templar agreed to protect relics in the west, while the Order of Saladin secured several relics to the east. These two noble orders would band together over the centuries for a series of 'hidden' crusades against the forces of evil that escaped the Disjunction.

My History

My direct male forebearer, Sir Michael of Carrington, fought in the 3rd Crusade at Acre at this battle.

This family story may well have been this history that has been kept hidden until now. The crest he carried into battle at Acre was the Unicorn (symbol of Ephraim) and the crown (royal lineage) placed over the neck of the unicorn.

Many Wars in History

Wars against the Nephilim have been fought in the days of Cain (circa 4000 BC), the days of Noah and Enoch at the time of the great flood (circa 2300 BC), the days of Abraham and Melchizedek/ Shem (circa 1500 BC), by Moses in Egypt (circa 1200 BC), by King David in the land of Israel (circa 1000 BC) , By Jesus on the cross and His Church (circa 34 AD), by King Arthur (circa 580 AD) in Britain and by King Richard (circa 1100 AD) in the Holy Land.

The war of the seed of the god-man Adam against the Nephilim is not over but continues into this modern era. We will soon see all of the forces of the universe (including alien species) involved in these future battles on earth.

Spiritual First

To reemphasize a truth, the battle is first spiritual and then occurs in the natural or physical realm.

Most of the battles that I now fight are fought in my sleep and recorded in my dreams. Technology cannot save the world – only faith in the true Messiah who empowers his armies to be 'overcomers' by the "blood of the lamb [Y'Shua] and the word of their testimony [holy living]" will work. This we can be assured of as the faithful of YHWH prepare for battle.

21. Dream-Vision: Bunker for the Faithful

Underground Dwellings

Just before falling asleep on the 30th of December, 2007, I found myself aloft over the Rocky Mountains in the Colorado region. As I looked down upon the vast range, I saw hundreds of little black dotes scattered among the mountains and valleys going from the Southern US all the way up into Canada.

I then found myself moving closer and I was able to see through the dense forests and saw that the dots were actually shadows. As I moved closer still, the shadows became entrances to caves, tunnels and man-made underground dwellings. I then understood that it was in these places that the people of the Lord would be protected.

Why Underground

Now awake, I wondered why would underground be important to be safe from the oppression of the NWO-UN military. I then remembered the capability of satellite imagery. Such technologies are very advanced and a person in the middle of the forest can be found if they are on the surface of the ground.

The technologies include 1) light enhanced imagery, 2) motion detection, 3) object/form detection (avoid squares), 4) radar detection, 5) metals detection, 6) density detection (underground), 7) infrared detection and 8) sound detection.

To avoid being seen by these technologies, the safest place is underground with at least a 6' layer of earth or rock above to separate you from the view of satellites. The bunkers need to be kept small so density or cavity detection is minimized. I suggest a maximum of about 12' in the round (not square) as the largest space.

Even vehicles need to be stored underground.

An easy way to build underground is to fill burlap bags with soil/sand/gravel that you have dug from the site and add some Portland cement (dry), mix together and simple stack overlapping the bags. Natural moisture will activate the cement and harden it.

Also run 2 strands of barbed wire between the rows of bags to lock them together. The roof can be made of cut trees of about 8" and larger placed side by side over the whole roof area. Then add a strong plastic waterproofing tarp over the top with 2' of earth on top of all. Entrances should be difficult to see - hidden behind trees or brush.

Food is a serious concern for emergency remote living. I would suggest choosing locations that have natural springs (water coming from the ground - not a stream) and a store of winter wheat and other grains be placed at each location. The wheat and grains can be sprouted in a few days to provide most of the nutrients needed to live. Hunting game to supplement is suggested.

January 1, 2014 update

I now understood that these shelter locations will also become a safe haven for animals because it will provide shelter and water for them. Vehicles will become a burden and not an asset as the siege continues to find and incarcerate true believers. The animals seek peace and as the end comes near, there will be no peace on the earth. Wild animals will gravitate to where there is still a spirit of peace, water, food, shelter and perhaps salt-minerals for their consumption. The once ferocious beast will become a friend to the faithful as guardians.

22. Dream-Vision: US Invasion Imminent

Canada-US Border

I was greatly disturbed as I slept on a night in December 2007. I was then partially awakened and found myself hovering above the Canada - US border near Montana looking down upon the border. I was called 'Windwalker' in this encounter by my spirit host (angel?) as the facts were revealed.

As I looked down at the border (about mid-US on the map) a word was spoken to me. An angel said,

"There are 600,000 NWO-UN forces at the Border now ready to invade the U.S."

Yes... this is not a typo.... the number stated as 600,000.

Tunnels for Invasion

Then I saw multiple tunnels underground along the Border that penetrated deep into US territory as hidden underground highways to be used for the invasion. I strongly understood the invasion was imminent and the time table for the invasion was moved-up (sooner) than what was previously planned due to some international incident that will soon be revealed by the media. I was greatly disturbed by this in my Spirit. I then was fully awakened.

I now understand the title Windwalker was to represent a group of prophet-seers that will hear and foretell what is to come upon the world before it happens. I was counted among this group. This is to provide to the Church the opportunity to be ready and not be caught unaware of the difficulties to come.

Since I find myself often among a group of viewers, I am therefore only one among many Windwalkers who are of the School of the Prophets who are being communicated with by YHWH in these last days.

The NWO-UN military forces along the Canada-US border according to Internet sources (perhaps valid) are primarily UN forces comprised of E. German, Russian and Chinese military. It is also noted from Internet sources that there are two transportation tunnels already built under the sea between Russia and Alaska and the others between Siberia and Canada.

The southern Border has NWO-UN military primarily comprised of Mexican, Middle Eastern and S. American personnel. The tunnels provide a covert and sudden invasion capability for a very large military force that can takeover the major cities along the border. It may also provide access to US train terminals (in train yard warehouses) to load military personnel into trains to be quietly transported to cities farther south of the Canadian border.

The whole invasion could occur within a 24 hour period or even in one night as we sleep. It is believed that Martial Law will concurrently be instituted by the President and the NWO/UN forces will be described as 'peace-keeping' forces to assist with Martial Law.

National ID

A 'national' ID of all people in the US using the ID Chip will be required so the government can determine your whereabouts anywhere in the US. The ID Chip has been approved for use in all new passports for travel in the US, Canada, Caribbean and Mexico. This suggests Martial Law and an ID will be provided within all of these countries who are members of the North American Trade Agreement.

Another act of the President to shortly follow will be to command the NWO-UN forces under Martial Law to go house to house to confiscate ALL weapons and firearms to assure peace under Martial Law. The international incident that will be used to justify Martial Law is not known to me at this time. My sense is that it will be of greater devastation than the 9-11 incident in the US.

Based on what I am seeing, I would recommend not living in the large US cities. Rather, move out into the country where you can grow/raise your own food and be off-grid from utility companies.

23. Tabernacle of David

The liturgy of the Tabernacle of David is prophesied in the Scriptures to return to earth in the end times. It is placed here in the Field Manual as a liturgy of preparation for battle that can be used personally or assisted by Culdee Chaplains when in training and during deployment. It was customary for knights all through history to participate in a liturgy or ritual to cleanse their souls of sin and to commit themselves to YHWH to be their protector in battle.

The liturgy of the Tabernacle of David is literally the putting on of the Armor of YHWH to be ready to fight spiritual battles. It includes the 7 Tabernacle steps aligned with the 7 pieces of armor that protects the mind (Helmet of Salvation), the heart (Breastplate of Righteousness), the loins (Belt of Truth), the legs/feet (Shoes of the Preparation of the Gospel of Peace). Added to this is the offensive weapons welded by the arms including the Shield of Faith and the Sword of the Spirit.

The core of this battle liturgy dates to the first century AD and was used prior to 50 AD in Jerusalem. It was the first liturgy based on the events of the Upper Room in which Y'Shua said, "as often as you do this, do this in remembrance of me." It is the first Eucharist or communion used by the New Testament Church prior to the influence of Greek and Roman paganism that corrupted the new church by 325 AD under Constantine.

Tabernacle of David Vision

In the evening of the 3rd of November, 2015, I was in much prayer through the day seeking direction. I was at the Hopi Reservation in Arizona and seeking a means to connect with the native people. I then had a vision of the Tabernacle of David.

Yes... the Tabernacle of David and not the Tabernacle of Moses. It was greatly reduced in size from that of Moses and was easily carried in a small truck. The Holy of Holies was not more than 10' by 10' and 10' tall and made of light pipe construction with curtains on all 4 sides.

The furniture of this Tabernacle was more representational and not intended for full use as in the Tabernacle of Moses since no blood sacrifice was to occur.

1. The Gate of Entry was just a pipe arch.
2. The Altar was a small BBQ on legs.
3. The Lavor was a large bowel cradled on a stand.
4. The Table of Shewbread was no more than 2' by 3' with communion elements thereon.
5. The Menorah was about 5' tall with the 7 candles alight in glass votive holders.
6. The Censor was a thurable that was hanging on a hook stand pressed into the ground.
7. When entering into the Holy of Holies through the curtain, the Ark was a box 1.5' by 3' on a portable stand with the two angels on the lid of the box facing each other.

I was then told,

"You are David the son of David and you are to serve in the Tabernacle of David as a priest of David to my people."

In hearing this, I knew it was the Order of Melchizedek that was meant by the phrase, 'priest of David'. Y'Shua is now the high priest of this most ancient Holy order that began with Adam in the Garden of Eden. About two years ago, I was told by YHWH to "no longer be an Orthodox, or an Episcopalian, or a Catholic or a Franciscan but only be of the Order of Melchizedek."

I have since withdrawn from all of these groups. I am now only a Culdee which is the Celtic version of the School of the Prophets and means literally "one who is a friend of God."

I then went to the Holy Scriptures to find references to the Tabernacle of David and the last days. This is what I found.

> After this I [Y'Shua] will return, and will build again the tabernacle of David, which is fallen down; and I will build again the ruins thereof, and I will set it up. Acts 15:16

> But after I uproot them, I will again have compassion and will bring each of them back to their own inheritance and their own country. Jeremiah 12:15

> "In that day I will restore David's fallen shelter [Tabernacle] I will repair its broken walls and restore its ruins-- and will rebuild it as it used to be. Amos 9:11

This Tabernacle of David is definitely planned by YHWH for the last days in the reestablishing of the Tabernacle of David and this as a gathering sign for his people in preparation for a return to the land of Israel. It will continue to exist into the Millennium and as it appears by this vision, we are to begin now as we enter into the time of Jacob's trouble to gather together the faithful of the seed of Jacob for a return to their homeland in Israel.

What was interesting about this Tabernacle is that it did not have the curtains around the holy place where the Table, Menorah and Censor were located. Nor were the Gate, Altar and Lavor separate from these other pieces just mentioned.

Only the Ark had its own place separate from the rest in this Tabernacle of David. The six pieces of furniture were all visually seen and accessible by the masses who wanted to worship YHWH. Only the Holy of Holies still had the curtain and even this was open to the front for access by all who dared enter therein. I say dared since an unrepentant person near the Ark resulted in instant death in the past.

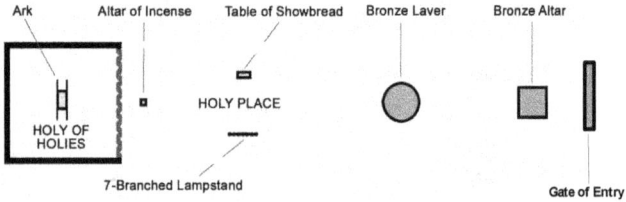

If I am to build an Ark, what am I to put in the Ark I wondered? Certainly the bible. Perhaps Oil and Water for anointing. Perhaps the bread and wine for communion. All of these are the symbols of our covenant with YHWH as made possible by Y'Shua who shed his blood upon the cross.

Chapter 24: Liturgy of the Tabernacle of David

Compiled from Ante-Nicene sources by Abbot-Bishop David Michael, OC as modeled to us by Moses and David in the Tabernacle

The minister reads all plain font words while the congregation reads the bold font words in response or in confession. Rubrics are in smaller italicized indented font.

Gate of Thanksgiving: Cloak of Humility

The units enter into the Sanctuary early and leave their tithes, offerings and Eucharistic gifts at a designated place at the back of the Sanctuary.

The following scripture from Matt 5:23-24 may be recited by the communicants at the entrance to the Sanctuary or place of worship.

Jesus taught us saying, "Therefore, if thou bring thy gift to the Altar, and there rememberest that thy brother hast ought against thee; Leave there thy gift before the Altar, and go thy way; First be reconciled to thy brother, and then come and offer thy gift."

Each unit may sing a song or recite a psalm in praise to God as they enter and leave their gift. Upon entering, each unit may sit or kneel and pray until they are ready to approach the Altar of Forgiveness.

When all are finished, the minister may say the following.

It is the humble that shall inherit the earth and we are all given a cloak of humility by God. Let us put on that cloak of humility as we prepare our hearts in prayer for battle.

Altar of Forgiveness: Belt of Truth

The Decalogue may be recited in each unit as led by a Knight, the Knight Commander or a Chaplain or recited together in a gathering.

God spoke these words and said:

I am the Lord thy God; Thou shalt have none other gods but me.

Lord have mercy upon us, and incline our hearts to keep this law.

Thou shalt not make to thyself any graven image, nor the likeness of anything that is in heaven above, or in the earth beneath, or in the water under the earth; thou shalt not bow down to them, nor worship them.

Lord have mercy upon us.

Thou shalt not take the name of the Lord thy God in vain.

Lord have mercy upon us.

Remember that thou keep holy the Sabbath day.

Lord have mercy upon us, and incline our hearts to keep this law.

Honor thy father and thy mother;

Lord have mercy upon us.

Thou shalt do no murder.
Lord have mercy upon us, and incline our hearts to keep this law.

Thou shalt not commit adultery.

Lord have mercy upon us.

Thou shalt not steal.

Lord have mercy upon us.

Thou shalt not bear false witness against thy neighbor.

Lord have mercy upon us, and incline our hearts to keep this law.

Thou shalt not covet.

Lord have mercy upon us, and incline our hearts to keep this law.

Prayer of Confession

Each member that is a communicant is to draw near to the Altar where there is a fire burning. Each baptized Christian may take a piece of paper provided and write upon the paper any sins they may have committed since last confession. The penitent says a personal prayer of confession asking Y'Shua to forgive their sin by his blood as the paper is put into the fire and burned up. When all have finished, the minister says:

Let us pray the general prayer of confession for our sins.

Lord, we have sinned and come short of your glory for what we have done and for what we have left undone. We are not worthy to be your children. Please forgive us. With repentant hearts, we ask to be reconciled in renewed fellowship with you dear Father YaHuVeh through the shed blood of Y'Shua your son. Empower us by your Holy Spirit to be overcomers in this world and examples of your great love to all creation. May your holy law become our Belt of Truth that saves us from evil. In the name of the +Father, the +Son and the +Holy Spirit. Amen.

The minister will then approach the Altar to pray for all penitents to receive God's forgiveness and absolution.

Be you forgiven of your sins through the blood of Jesus and go and sin no more in the name of the +Father , the +Son and +Holy Spirit. Amen.

> *When finished, the minister leads the units in the 'Our Father' which may be sung together as a congregation.*

Let us pray together...

Our Father, who are't in heaven, hallowed be thy Name. Thy Kingdom come. Thy will be done, on earth as it is in heaven. Give us this day our daily bread and forgive us our trespasses, as we forgive those that trespass against us. And lead us not into temptation, but deliver us from evil. Amen.

Laver of Confession: Breastplate of Righteousness

> *The minister now moves near the Laver that is filled with water.*

> *The weekly readings of the Holy Scriptures are to be read to the gathering at this time according to a cycle of the readings as chosen by the Abbot General. Preaching and teaching may follow the readings as the Holy Spirit leads.*

> *The minister may 'sprinkle' the communicants with Holy Water, as symbolic of their receiving of the Word and its cleansing action, following the readings. Foot washing and Baptisms may also occur on special occasions during this time.*

> *Upon the completion of the readings and teachings, the Apostles Creed is to be prayed by the communicants.*

Let us together confess our faith through the Apostles Creed.

I believe in God the Father almighty, Maker of heaven and earth. And in Y'Shua our Messiah his first born son our Lord: Who was conceived by the Holy Ghost, born of the virgin Mary; suffered under Pontius Pilate, was crucified, dead and buried: He descended into hell;

The third day he rose again from the dead: He ascend into heaven, and sitteth on the right hand of the Father Almighty: from thence he shall come to judge the quick and the dead.

I believe in the Holy Ghost: The holy one church; the communion of saints; the forgiveness of sins; the resurrection of the body; and the life everlasting. Amen.

Lord may we take on this creed of confession as our Breastplate of Righteousness in holding fast to the faith given to us by Y'Shua and the holy Apostles.

Amen.

Table of Covenant: Shoes of Peace

> *The minister then moves near the Table. Songs may be presented at this time in preparation for communion. Only baptized believers may partake in the Eucharist.*
>
> *The minister will call the people together with a warning that they must partake of the Body and Blood of our Lord with understanding, having confessed their sins and having been reconciled with God and their brethren. The minister will consecrate the elements by the sign of the cross so they become the Body and Blood of our Lord Messiah Y'Shua. (Corinthians 11:23-27)*
>
> *From the Didache of circa 96 AD As regards the cup:*

We give Thee thanks, O our Father, for the holy vine of Thy son David, which Thou madest known unto us through Thy Son Y'Shua;

Thine is the glory for ever and ever.

Then as regards the broken bread:

We give Thee + thanks, O our Father, for the life and knowledge which Thou didst make known unto us through Thy Son Y'Shua;

Thine is the glory for ever and ever.

As this broken bread was scattered upon the mountains and being gathered together became one, so may thy faithful be gathered together from the ends of the earth into Thy kingdom; for

Thine is the glory and the power through Y'Shua Messiah for ever and ever.

But let no one eat or drink of this Eucharist thanksgiving, but they that have been baptized into the name of the Y'Shua our Messiah; for concerning this also the Lord hath said: "Give not that which is holy to the dogs."

We give Thee thanks, Holy Father, for Thy holy name, which Thou hast made your Tabernacle of David in our hearts, and for the knowledge and faith and immortality, which Thou hast made known unto us through thy Son Y'Shua;

Thine is the glory for ever and ever.

Thou, Almighty Master, didst create all things for Thy name's sake, and didst give food and drink unto men for enjoyment, that they might render thanks to Thee; but didst bestow upon us spiritual food and drink and eternal life through thy Son. Before all things we give thee thanks that Thou art powerful;

Thine is the glory for ever and ever.

Remember, Lord, Thy Church [and warriors] to deliver it from all evil and to perfect it in Thy love; and [gather it together from the four winds]-- even the Church which has been sanctified into Thy kingdom which Thou hast prepared for it; for

Thine is the power and the glory for ever and ever.

May grace come and may this world pass away. Hosanna to the God of David. If any man is holy, let him come; if any man is not, let him repent.

Maranatha.

For I have received from the Lord what I have also delivered unto you, that the Lord Y'Shua the same night in which he was betrayed took bread. And when he had given thanks+, he brake it, and said,

"Take eat; this is my body, which is broken for you+; this do in remembrance of me."

> *Celebrant will say a prayer of consecration over the bread and break the bread lifting it before heaven.*

After the same manner also he took the cup, when he had supped, saying,

"This cup is the New Testament in my blood+; this do ye, as oft as ye drink it, in remembrance of me."

> *Celebrant will say a prayer of consecration over the wine and mix the wine with water lifting it before heaven. Then holding up both the bread and wine before heaven, he will say.*

For as often as you eat this bread and drink this cup, ye do show the Lord's death 'til he come.

> *Celebrant will now distribute the elements. He may say "the bread of heaven" as he distributes the bread. He may say "the cup of salvation" as he distributes the wine. He will then close with the following prayer.*

Let us pray together.

Lord God, may we bring peace into this world with the Shoes of Peace that others may see the fellowship of our love one for another. From this love, may the unsaved be drawn to you and become your people. Amen.

Menorah of Revelation: Shield of Faith

> *The minister moves near to the Menorah and lights the seven candles.*
>
> *The seven candles of the Menorah [chapter 11] are referring to the Messiah as the Branch. They are the, 1) Spirit of the Lord, 2) Spirit of Knowledge, 3) Spirit of Understanding, 4) Spirit of Wisdom, 5) Spirit of Might, 6) Spirit of Counsel and the 7) Spirit of the Fear of the Lord [reverence]. Faith comes by hearing and hearing by the word (logos and rhema) of God.*

And there shall come forth a rod out of the Stem of Jesse and a Branch shall grow out of his roots. And the Spirit of the Lord shall rest upon him, the Spirit of Wisdom and Understanding, the Spirit of Counsel and Might, the Spirit of Knowledge and the Fear of the Lord

And shall make him of quick understanding in the fear of the Lord; and he shall not judge after the sight of his eyes neither reprove after the hearing of his ears. But with righteousness shall he judge the poor, and reprove with equity for the meek of the earth.

Let us pray together.

Lord God. You are the source of all wisdom and knowledge. Enlighten our hearts by your life-giving revelation that comes by the ministry of the Holy Spirit. Make your will in us our Shield of Faith and teach us that we may likewise go and teach others to hear and to obey your holy word. Amen.

I invite a person from each unit to come and light a candle and set it before the Menorah to show their desire as a unit to receive a word from the heart of God.

> *The minister will then encourage each of the units to pray together to receive a revelation from the Lord and to later share the revelation with the others in their unit for confirmation from the prophets.*

Censor of Intercession: Sword of the Spirit

> *The minister moves near the Censor and prepares to incense the people of God and then prays as he is incensing the people.*

Almighty Lord, receive the prayers of your people as the Sword of the Spirit that divides between soul and spirit. In the name of the +Father, the +Son and the +Holy Spirit.

Amen.

> *The people or a choir may sing during this time.*
> *Receiving revelation and confirmation, the units who have*
> *gathered may then pray together as one voice and heart. Each*
> *unit is encouraged to have someone pray according to the*
> *revelation that was given to their unit. As the prayers are*
> *being said, the censor is carried throughout the units*
> *gathered with incense being dispersed symbolizing the*
> *prayers of the people of God that rise into the heavenlies.*

Ark of Fellowship: Helmet of Salvation

Let us pray together

Lord God, may we become known as the "Friends of God" and take on the Helmet of Salvation that fills our lives with joy, peace and love. Amen.

Let us now enjoy the feast of fellowship in his presence. Go in peace to Love and serve the Lord.

Thanks be to God

> *Following the prayers, informal worship may follow in joyful*
> *song and dance. All may share in this worship in singing*
> *and playing instruments of music. This is also a time of*
> *eating (if appropriate) and enjoying each others friendship*
> *and friendship with God.*

25. Printed and Web Sources

Reading required for the Knights, Sergeants and Soldiers of the Order of the Gate includes the four books written by Abbot David, Abbot General of the Order of the Gate. In addition to these books is the School of the Prophets series just now being published. These books provide an in-depth understanding in exposing the powers behind the powers operating in these final wars of good against evil.

The titles of the four books include:

2015 Alien Invasion	ISBN# 978-0615776385
2015 Draconian NWO	ISBN# 978-0615806679
2015 Nephilim Wars	ISBN# 978-0615845616
2015 Melchizedek Arises	ISBN# 978-0692268490

In addition, the title of the two books for chaplain-prophets include:

Prophets I: Origin
Propehts II: Unity

And more books ..... with KINDLE versions of these books now available!

Books published by Glentivar Village Press and printed by Create Space: http://createspace.com.can be ordered through links from: http://glentivar.org

If you want to order 10 or more copies, a discount code can be provided to you for this purchase. Contact Abbot David directly at: info@glentivar.org for the discount code.

Other questions and correspondence concerning the Order or the content of his books may also be sent to Abbot David at info@glentivar.org

Information about Saint Michaels Abbey as the home for the Order of the Gate, Order of the Culdee and as the School of the Prophets can be viewed at http://schooloftheprophets.us.

As a chaplain, the skills in music to speak/sing the language of the forces of nature including the armies of the 4 winds can be found at: http://battleharp.com.

Abbot David Michael, ThD
Abbot General, 1993-present.
Order of the Culdee (Chaplains)
Order of the Gate (Knights)